Spiritual
POETRY

Spiritual POETRY

POETRY *for the* MIND, BODY, *and* SOUL!

ANNETTE SILER

XULON PRESS

Xulon Press
555 Winderley Pl, Suite 225
Maitland, FL 32751
407.339.4217
www.xulonpress.com

© 2024 by Annette Siler

All rights reserved solely by the author. The author guarantees all contents are original and do not infringe upon the legal rights of any other person or work. No part of this book may be reproduced in any form without the permission of the author.

Due to the changing nature of the Internet, if there are any web addresses, links, or URLs included in this manuscript, these may have been altered and may no longer be accessible. The views and opinions shared in this book belong solely to the author and do not necessarily reflect those of the publisher. The publisher therefore disclaims responsibility for the views or opinions expressed within the work.

Unless otherwise indicated, Scripture quotations taken from the King James Version (KJV)–*public domain.*

Paperback ISBN-13: 979-8-86850-294-1
Ebook ISBN-13: 979-8-86850-295-8

ACKNOWLEDGMENTS

First and forever, I thank God for blessing me and giving me the gift to write His Word for all who read, believe, and receive it! Thank you to my son, Reggie, who has been with me every step of the way, even when he had to go through his surgeries and recoveries. Thank you to my daughter, Briana, and my niece, Alexis, who helped me to type each poem for this awesome spiritual poetry book. I would like to give a thankful shoutout to my pastors, Willie and Annie Blackmon. Their sermons were filled with Word from our God and a lot of those blessed poems are from those powerful, eye-opening Words of God. I thank all who will get a copy of my poetry book, read it, be blessed by it, and know that we serve an awesome, loving, merciful, healing, and supernatural God!

TABLE OF CONTENTS

1. He is God! 1
   - Are you Sick? 3
   - Committed to the Journey............................ 4
   - Don't Stress It; Let God Bless It!..................... 5
   - Don't Sweat It; God's Got It!......................... 6
   - Get Plugged into God................................ 7
   - God, Get Up in My Face! 8
   - "God's Got This." 9
   - Heal Me, My Healer! 10
   - It's What God Says that Counts! 11
   - Just Don't Quit!..................................... 12
   - Just Like That!...................................... 13
   - Keep Your Love Right............................... 14
   - Kick Up the Praise! 15
   - Learn to Suffer Well! 16
   - Let God Arise! 17
   - Let Love Lead the Way.............................. 18
   - "You cannot serve God and mammon."............... 19
   - Numbers 23:19...................................... 20
   - Obey and Worship God!............................. 21

    Perhaps You have Heard these Proverbs?............ 23
    Praise Your Way Out!............................. 24
    Rest in the Lord................................. 25
    Soaking Wet!..................................... 26
    Speak the Word!.................................. 27
    Submit and Resist!............................... 28
    Take God out of the Box!......................... 29
    The Blessed Shall Remain Blessed................. 30
    The Kingdom is in You!........................... 31
    "The Lord is my Shepherd"........................ 32
    Trust God.. 33
    The Word of God!................................. 34
    When You Can't, God Can!......................... 35
    Your Miracle Comes Out of Your Mess.............. 36

2. His Name is Jesus.................................. 37
    Crucify that Flesh............................... 39
    Death to Self; Let Christ Live in You............ 40
    Do You Know Jesus?............................... 41
    Get Addicted to Jesus............................ 42
    Got Jesus?....................................... 43
    His Name is Jesus: A Skit........................ 44
    I Am the Door!................................... 47
    Jesus: He is Everything that We Need!............ 48
    Jesus, I Will Never Forget....................... 50
    Jesus Makes Life Better!......................... 51
    Jesus: Our Hope is in You........................ 52
    Jesus, Our Savior................................ 53

Jesus Said it: That's Enough. 54
Jesus!. 55
Leaning on Jesus. 56
Stand for Christ.. 57
They Just Don't Know. 58
What a Price He Paid!. 59

3. Salvation 61
Priceless. 63
How Can I Hear You?. 65
Not only Forgiven, but Forgotten.. 66
Break it Down.. 67
Salvation is for All.. 68
Now Is the Time for Salvation.. 69
Repent, God Wants You To. 70
Salvation: Do you Accept this Free Gift? 72
Salvation, God's Gift to You.. 73
Saved is the Way. 74
Say What You Believe; Believe What You Say. 75
Seven Steps to Salvation.. 76
Will You be Ready? 77

4. Faith 79
Faith. 81
Fight to Win.. 82
Get a Grip! 83
Standing on Your Faith. 84
When Faith Shows Up. 85
The Power of Faith. 86

Choose Not to Faint!...........................88
Looking Through the Eyes of Faith..............89
Build Your House on the Rock...................90
Life: Living in Faith Every Day.................91
Stop and Pause.................................92
Faith to Hold On...............................93

5. Pray..95
Give Out, but Not Giving In....................97
He Lives! (*a play*)...........................98
If You Don't Pray, You Won't Stay.............103
Jesus Prayed!.................................104
Pray, Press, and Praise!......................106
Press and Pray!...............................107
You've Got to Pray!...........................108

6. The Devil is a Liar..........................109
Devil, I Am Not Coming Down...................111
Devil, I Am Not for Sale......................112
Don't Let Sin Sneak Back In...................113
Don't Take the Bait (of Satan)................114
Don't Buy the Lie.............................115
Don't Go to Hell from the Pew.................116
Show the Devil the Door.......................117
"Sin Ain't Your Friend."......................118
Sin is Like a Bag of Smelly Garbage...........119
Take Heed, Don't be Deceived..................120
The Devil is a Liar...........................121
The Flesh is a Mess!..........................122

7. Get Your Mind in Line! 123
   Don't be Derailed. 125
   Get Wisdom; Get Understanding. 126
   Get Your Mind in Line. 128
   Grow Up! 129
   Hearing Mess Will Mess You Up. 130
   How Can I Hear You? 131
   I've Got to Get This Right. 132
   Isaiah 1:19. 133
   It's About the Thought Life. 134
   Mind Under Construction. 135
   Perhaps You Have Heard These Proverbs? 136
   Swat It Off (Let It Go). 138
   What Are You Saying? 139
   Wise Up. 140

8. Christmas Poetry 141
   A Christmas Miracle. (*a play*) 143
   A Christmas Miracle. 150
   A Christmas Welcome. 151
   We Bow Down. 152
   Picture This. 153
   Signs, Wonders, and Miracles, Oh My! 154
   The Perfect Gift. 155
   Christmas Time. 156
   Christmas: The Savior is Born. 157

9. Easter 159
   Christ Got Up! 161

He Lives! 162
An Easter Welcome. 163
Jesus is Alive! 164
Good News. 165
He Lives! 166
He was Born; He Died; and He has Risen!. 167
In Three Days. 169

10. Miscellaneous Poetry. 171
Salute the "Real" Dads. 173
A Woman of Few Words. 174
Dead Man Walking.. 175
Fathers. 176
Guard Your Heart. 177
"I Don't!" Until We Say, "I Do!" 178
Moms. 179
Mothers. 180
What My Daughter Said.. 181
WHAT IF? (*a play*) 182

HE IS GOD!

Are You Sick?

Are you sick? Are you ready to give up, throw in the towel? Here are some scriptures full of God's healing words and power.
Isaiah 53:5: "But he was wounded for our transgressions, he was bruised for our iniquities: the chastisement of our peace was upon him; and with his stripes we are healed."
Trust God to heal you; this is a non-changing faithful deal.
Psalms 6:2: "Have mercy upon me, O Lord; for I am weak: O Lord, heal me; for my bones are vexed."
Touch me Lord, let your healing power get me soaking wet!
Jeremiah 17:14: "Heal me, O Lord, and I shall be healed;"
Call out to God; He heals and prints out no bill!
Luke 17:19: "And he said unto him, Arise, go thy way: thy faith hath made thee whole."
Faith brings Jesus on the scene; believe and receive your healing from the top of your head to the tips of your toes.
Psalms 30:2: "O Lord, my God, I cried unto thee, and thou hast healed me."
Yes, a small cry to the Lord, and He will hear and heal thee.
James 5:16: "Confess your faults one to another, and pray one for another, that ye may be healed. The effectual fervent prayer of a righteous man availeth much."
That righteous prayer one for another will reach out and bring God's healing touch.
Listen, trust, believe, and receive! God's healing is faithful, strong, and real.
Don't let your sicknesses and diseases cloud your mind and steal your supernatural heal!

Committed to the Journey.

Commit thy way unto the Lord; trust also in Him, and He shall bring it to pass.
Commit to the journey; trouble may come but it won't always last.
Commit to the journey; God will direct you.
He will lead you in everything that you say or do.
Commit to the journey; it won't always be to your understanding.
You may find this journey to be somewhat demanding.
Commit to the journey; you must trust and faithfully move.
When you follow God's directions, you will not lose.
Commit to the journey; God is already ahead of you.
Yes, your journey can lead to blessings and increase too.
Commit to the journey; do what you must.
Follow God's directions, walk in faithful trust.
Commit to the journey; it sometimes feels like a long relay.
Continue to follow God's directions, commit, and obey.
Commit to the journey; get in that race.
Follow God's directions; you need to walk or run a faith filled and calming pace.
Commit to the journey; God will order your steps.
Follow God's directions; it can also lead to your wealth.
Commit to the journey; just go forth, open your eyes.
Follow God's directions, stand strong and rise!

Don't stress it; Let God bless it!

Jesus died on the cross; He hung from a tree.
His sacrificial gift was given to set us free.
The devil wants us to fall into his pit.
Don't stumble, don't stress it; Let God bless it!
Things don't always go your way.
Don't stress it; Let God bless it: open deaf ears, and listen to what He has to say.
There will be times when you will pout and cry.
Don't stress it; Let God bless it: He will dry the tears and give you holy wings to fly!
Don't stress it; Let God bless it: receive His peace,
Then all doubts, pouts and discord will cease!
Be strong in the power of His might.
Don't stress it; Let God bless it: you can win this faith fight.
Sometimes friends will make promises that they can't or won't keep.
Don't stress it; Let God bless it: His friendship is true and runs deep!
Don't stress it; Let God bless it: stand strong.
God is always there; He will never leave you alone.
Don't stress the trials, don't stress the tests.
Let God bless it: He will give you His peaceful rest.
Don't stress it; Let God bless it: He is watching and sending His angels to surround and protect you!
Ask, seek, and knock; Get ready for what He is about to do!
Get God's words in your spirit; be faithful and bold.
Don't stress it; Let God bless it: for to Him, you are more precious and valuable than silver and gold!

Don't Sweat It; God's got It!

The bills are due, your creditors won't wait.
They are threatening to take it all if you are one month late.
No one wants to give you a break.
The lights are about to be cut off; your faith begins to shake.
Suddenly among all the turmoil and stress,
A scripture flashes through your mind during this test.
Philippians 4:19: "My God shall supply all your needs."
We must keep on pressing and sowing those seeds!
Sometimes darkness will come and block the light.
It is during these times that we must hold on to faith and fight.
Don't sweat it; God's got it! Don' question why.
Just know that "he is not a man that he should lie."
He knows and sees everything that we go through.
He is not looking at what you see, but what you do.
Don't sweat it; God's got it! You must believe.
You can ask anything in Jesus' name, and you will receive!

Get Plugged into God.

Someone asked this question, "What do you do when you are feeling down and low?"
I answered, "This is not good, for these emotions will block God's flow."
"Your heart will get heavier and your flesh becomes weak.
These emotions will lead to feelings of depression and defeat!"
"Sleep will leave and take its peace.
All blessings will seem to cease!"
"That devil will draw near and stick closer than a friend.
It won't even bother you when he glides you back to sin!"
"There is a cure, and it can come quick.
You need Jesus, you are spiritually sick!"
"Get plugged into God; pray your way out.
He is the break-through power that you need, there is no doubt!"
"Don't buddy up with the devil, he is the wrong one.
Resist him, he will flee! Let God's will be done!"
Get plugged into God! He will give you a powerful boost!
Now get up, praise Him, and shake yourself loose!

God, Get up in My Face!

God, oh, my rock, get up in my face.
I need your help to win this race.
God, Heavenly Father, get up in my face; lead me to do right.
When you get up in my face, I can see the light.
God, Prince of Peace, get up in my face; let turmoil cease.
Send your anointing with its supernatural peace.
God, my salvation, get up in my face; save my soul.
Help me to stand strong, living faithful and bold.
God, the Lord of my life, get up in my face, rule, and reign.
If you get up in my face, I will never be the same.
God, my God, get up in my face and lead the way.
Do it, God, get up in my face, every single day!

God's Got This.

The devil comes to kill, steal, and destroy the faith in you.
Let me tell you what you need to do.
When he says that you can't make it, you will die.
Tell him, "God's got this!" I know you lie!
When he tells you, your bills won't be paid.
Tell him, "God's got this!" He is my provider; I got it made!
When he tries to bring you fear and pain,
Tell him, "God's got this!" The God in me reigns!
When he comes to mess with your mind,
Tell him, "God's got this!" His peace is always on time!
The devil won't quit; he will never give up.
Neither will you; tell him, "God's got this!" The Lord fills my cup!

Heal Me, My Healer!

Psalms 6:2: "Have mercy upon me, O Lord, for I am weak: O Lord, heal me, for my bones are vexed."
Touch me Lord, let your healing power get me soaking wet!
Psalms 30:2: "O Lord my God, I cried unto thee, and thou hast healed me."
Cry out to God, your healer; He will heal thee!
Jeremiah 17:14: "Heal me O Lord, and I shall be healed;"
Call on the Lord for He heals and prints out no bills!
Isaiah 55:5: "But he was wounded for our transgressions, he was bruised for out iniquities: the chastisement of our peace was upon him; and with his stripes we are healed."
Trust God! This is a non-changing faithful deal!
James 5:16: "Confess your faults one to another, and pray one for another, that ye may be healed. The effectual fervent prayer of a righteous man availeth much."
Righteous prayer one for another will reach out and bring His healing touch!
Luke 17:19: "And he said unto him, Arise, go thy way: thy faith has made thee whole."
Have faith, it will bring Jesus on the scene; He will lead you down that healing road!
We will listen, trust, believe and receive God's healing. It is faithful and real.
Don't let your sicknesses and diseases cloud your mind and steal your supernatural heal!

It's what God Says that Counts!

The world says, "We have all sinned, therefore it is okay. God understands."
God says, "The wage of sin is death; but the gift of God is eternal life through Jesus Christ our Lord."
The world says, "Your past will keep you from being saved, God won't forgive you."
God says, "There is no respect of persons with God."
The world says, "What you don't know can't hurt you."
God says, "My people are destroyed for lack of knowledge: because thou hast rejected knowledge."
The world says, "Go ahead, live your life to the fullest; you only live once."
God says, "Be not deceived; God is not mocked; for whatsoever a man soweth, that shall he also reap."
The world says, "God helps those who helps themselves."
God says, "Blessed is he that considereth the poor; the Lord will deliver him in time of trouble."
The world says, "God knows my heart, when I curse, he knows that I don't mean it. He knows that I am not a bad person."
God says, "But I say to you, that for every idle word man shall speak, they shall give account thereof in the day of judgement."
The world says when you look good, you feel good.
God says when you feel good (sanctified, redeemed, filled with the Holy Ghost) you look good!
The world says, "It doesn't take all of that. Those church folks are crazy."
God says, "But ye are a chosen generation, a royal priesthood, a holy nation, a peculiar people; that ye should shew forth the praises of him who called you out of darkness into his marvelous light."

Just Don't Quit!

When the tests, trials, and persecutions come, and you know they will.
Don't stress it, trust God, just chill.
When you feel bad, body aching with pain.
Your mind is going crazy, wondering: where is God's rain?
Reach out, cry out, have a Holy Ghost fit.
Trust God to renew your mind and your strength, just don't quit!
Don't give up, just don't quit, for weeping may endure for a night.
God's joy comes in the morning, and it will ignite the light in you.
Just don't quit; persevere, stand bold.
You will reap the thirty, sixty, and, yes, the hundred-fold.
We know that old devil is a conniving thief.
He loves to bring the sorrow and the grief.
Just don't quit, give a deaf ear to him and turn your back on sin.
Remember God's Word says, "We are conquerors, we win!"
Just don't quit; speak to that mountain: it has to move, be cast into the sea.
Use God's Word: it is the key.
His Word will unlock doors for you to walk through.
Just don't quit, for He will bless even the mustard seed faith in you.
Just don't quit; the race is not given to the swift, nor the strong, but
To the one who grabs hold and holds on.
We serve an awesome God; He will honor and do His part!
Just don't quit; invite Him into your heart!

Just Like That!

God gave us a covenant; He made a pact,
and he can do it, just like that!
You may be sick, your body under attack;
Just know that Jesus is the great physician, and he can heal you, just like that!
No money, a stack of bills, so much lack;
Don't you know God can bring you out, just like that!
You don't need a Bubba, Jerome, or a free-loading Jack.
God can bless you with a Holy Ghost Husband, just like that!
Just like that, you can be living large and debt-free.
Living a life of health, wholeness, blessings, and blessed prosperity!
Search the Word; read about all the miracles that He has done.
See how he always puts that devil on the run!
Take the time to sit with God, have a long chat.
He will draw closer to you, just like that!
Just like that, blessings can come and overtake you.
Always put God first in all that you do!
God's Word says, "We can have what we say;" this is a spiritual fact.
Speak His Word and see Him do it, just like that!

Keep your Love Right.

John 3:16: "For God so loved the world that he gave his only begotten son."
It was His love for us that His will be done.
God loved us so much; He took up the fight.
Now you know, He kept His love right.
God commands us to love one another.
For this covers the sins of spiritual sisters and brothers.
Keeping our love right helps to develop faith and trust.
It will build a foundation of love; this is a must.
Keep your love right; love never fails.
It is to be given freely; it is not for sale.
Keep your love right; be faithful in love.
Love takes work, but you do have help from above.
Keep your love right, centered on God; He will guide you.
It is not just what you say, but also what you choose to do.
Keep your love right: love God; love yourself.
And, yes, you must spiritually love everybody else.
If you walk by love and not by flesh and sight,
You will be able to keep your love right!

KICK UP THE PRAISE!

We kick up the praise to another level.
Oops, there goes another devil!
That's alright, 'cause all I can see
Is a toothless enemy staring at me.
He can't bite; all he can do is pinch.
Our faith is strong; we won't budge one inch!
We kick up the praise, the heat is on.
God is back on the top where he belongs.
Don't you know the devil came to steal and to kill?
Kick up the praise to an awesome God who reigns and is real.
Kick up the praise through every trial and test.
Open your spiritual eyes and watch our God give you his very best.
We kick up the praise, the devil is a liar.
We kick up the praise, higher and higher!
We kick up the praise, it's a beautiful sound.
We kick up the praise! The blessings are raining down!
Kick up the praise; tear down the walls.
Kick up the praise; rejoice as they fall.
Kick up the praise; show no fear.
For the praise of worship is music to God's anointed ear!
Kick up the praise to the awesome God we serve!
Give Him the kind of praise He so richly deserves!

Learn to Suffer Well!

Jesus prayed, "Lord, if it is thy will, take this cup from me."
Yet, He still accepted what must be!
He chose to obey and suffer well.
For he knew he had a battle to fight in hell!
We need to learn to suffer well during our times of going through.
Jesus had to learn to suffer well too!
The devil turns up the heat; it is his job.
Learn to suffer well; for your faith he seeks to rob!
Keep in mind that Jesus has broken every yoke.
Learn to suffer well, don't lose hope!
Think about John the Baptist and Paul, locked up in jail.
They learned to suffer well, not letting their faith fail!
Job, he suffered well, and he passed the test,
And then God showed up, raining down blessings and rest!
When we learn to suffer well, having done all, we stand.
God renews our strength, blesses, and fill our hands!
1st Peter 5:10, "After that ye have suffered awhile, make you perfect, stablish, strengthen, settle you."
Learn to suffer well! God will bless everything that you do!

Let God Arise!

We give it all to God, let Him arise.
He leads and guides us, opening our eyes.
We see that in Him, we can trust,
and of course, obeying is a must.
When we let God arise, He will supply every need;
but remember, we must sow those seeds.
God will come through for you every time.
Let Him arise and a supernatural God you will find!
Stay faithful to God's word; He will be faithful to you.
Let Him arise and you will see and be amazed at what He can do.
Psalm 34:19: "Many are the afflictions of the righteous: but the Lord delivereth him out of them all."
Let God arise; give Him a call!
Psalm 23:1: "The Lord is my shepherd; I shall not want."
Let God arise, for if you don't,
You will find yourself catering to the flesh.
Let God arise, avoid the mess!
Let God arise, do your part.
Let God arise, arise in your heart!
God wants to arise in our life every day,
And He will when we trust and allow Him to have His way!

Let Love Lead the Way.

1 John 4:8 says, "He that loveth not, knoweth not God; for God is love."
The greatest love is the one that we receive from above.
2 Corinthians 5:14: "For the love of Christ constraineth us."
Allow that love to shine, not grow hard, turning to rust.
Let love guide and lead the way; you can't go wrong.
God's love builds us up and makes us strong.
Let love lead the way; blessings will overtake you.
And God will rain down His favor over everything you put your hands to do.
John 13:34: "A new commandment I give unto you, that ye love one another; as I have loved you, that ye also love one another."
We are to show forth God's love to all, especially our saved sisters and brothers.
Let love lead the way; it will bring you out.
You will have a new praise and a new shout!
Hebrews 13:1: "Let brotherly love continue." It is God's command.
A word sent forth to all saints and sinners throughout the land.
Let love lead the way; plant some love seeds!
Now watch our loving God bless and meet your needs!

Matthew 6:24: "You cannot serve God and mammon."

You cannot serve God and mammon; mammon is another name for money.
Choose to serve God, not your money; He is the one who can lead you into a land flowing with milk and honey!
Proverbs 3:9: "Honor the Lord with the first fruits of all thine increase."
Don't be so quick to give God your leftovers and the least!
Malachi 3:8: "Will a man rob God? Yet ye have robbed me."
Now God must honor his word and put a curse on thee.
Don't fall in love with that money, can't you see?
Giving your way out is the key!
Deuteronomy 28:1: "Hearken diligently unto the voice of the Lord, to observe and do."
All that God has commanded you!
Blessed you shall be in the city and in the field.
For God will give you favor on every deal.
Deuteronomy 28:4: "Blessed shall be the fruit of thy body, and the fruit of thy ground."
Money shall increase and your mind too shall be sound!
Blessed shall thou be coming in and blessed coming out.
Observing and obeying God's word is what this blessing is all about!
Serve God, not your money; bring Him your first and your best.
Now get ready; you are about to blow up and be blessed!

Numbers 23:19.

Numbers 23:19: "God is not a man that he should lie."
He said it! You can trust and rely on His Word!
His Word is always aye and Amen!
When God says we win, we win!
God never lies, his words are promising and true.
What our God says, He will do!
Numbers 23:19 will surely open your eyes.
You will see that Satan is the father of lies!
Search the Bible, God's words; study it every day.
Now, will you listen to what God has to say?
Numbers 23:19: "God is not a man that he should lie."
His word is alive; it won't fail, it won't die!

Obey and Worship God!

Satan's objective is still to get man and woman to disobey God.
Even when we know that God watches over our soul
and our bod.
God has called us to obey His commands.
His simple ways should lead us to obey and worship Him
with the lifting of our hands.
Obey God and worship Him from a loving and giving heart.
Just using your head can sometimes keep you and God apart.
When we are saved and believe, we need to obey and
worship Him.
Disobedience and listening to the devil will cause your heart
and eyes to grow dim.
Obedience is learning to obey God and do what His
Word says.
Obedience and worship will lead you to do things God's way.
Obey and listen: God is speaking, and His words are
in control.
He will lead you down the obedient and worshipful road.
Heed His voice, obey and do.
Worship God, He will bless you.
Obey and worship God, He will give you his peace.
Ask Him to help you sleep that peaceful sleep; then the devil
will have to cease.
Satan seeks those who disobey and refuse God's will.
You see, he seeks to destroy when we walk by what we
see and feel.
Satan has his own devilish plan.
He seeks the ones who see no disobedience in being a false
woman or man.
Obey and worship God; your season will come to you.
Obedience and worship will guide and blesses you, too.

Obey and worship your way through!
God will step in and anoint you to succeed in all that you say and do.

Perhaps You have Heard these Proverbs?

Proverbs 1:7 says, "The fear of the Lord is the beginning of knowledge; but fools despise wisdom and instruction."
In other words, not fearing God is a path to mayhem and destruction.
Proverbs 3:13: "Happy is the man that findeth wisdom and the man that getteth understanding."
It will be easy for this man to do what God is commanding.
Proverbs 6:17 says, "The Lord hates a proud look, a lying tongue, and hands that shed innocent blood."
He is a God of peace and brotherly love.
Proverbs gives wise advice and ways to live right.
Proverbs 12:22 says, "Lying lips are abomination to the Lord: but they that deal truly are his delight."
Proverbs 10:12: "Hatred stirreth up strifes, but love covereth all sins."
When we love His way, we can't help but win.
Our mouths should not be used for cursing and then singing a praising song.
Proverbs 18:21 says, "Death and life are in the power of the tongue,"
Don't treat your sins lightly; listen to God's words.
He is talking to us through these proverbs!
I will leave in your heart these two.
Remember God loves and wants to save you.
Proverbs 28:13: "He that covereth his sins shall not prosper: but whoso confesseth and forsaketh them shall have mercy."
Proverbs 18:10: "The name of the Lord is a strong tower: the righteous runneth into it and is safe."

Praise Your Way Out!

We hear God's Word and read it every day,
but doubts and fears will still come our way.
Bills are piling up; money gets tight.
Now, you find yourself in a faith fight.
Don't let what you go through
grab hold of your mind and get the best of you.
Praise your way out!
This is what a faith walk is all about.
Sickness comes, it works on your flesh and makes you weak.
Praise your way out! God is the one to praise and seek.
Your flesh can also make you look and act like a fool.
It will have you strutting around, believing that without God,
you are too cool.
There will be times when the things you do may not work
out right.
Just praise your way out: by walking in faith and not
what you see.
Lift those hands up; praise your way out!
Trusting in God will give you a victory shout.
Your friends are busy, having so much to do.
Sometimes when you call on them, they can only spare a
minute or two.
You are left feeling sad and alone.
Praise your way out: to God you will always belong.
Praise your way out! God loves it!
Praise your way out; you and God are a perfect fit!
Praise your way out! Crucify that flesh.
Trust God to clean up your dirty mess.
Praise your way out: shout and confess it!
Praise your way out! God will hear you and bless it!

Rest in the Lord.

Rest in the Lord: trust Him in the fight.
Rest in the Lord: walk by faith, not by sight.
You need God's spiritual rest.
It is a time of refreshing through the trials and tests.
Rest in the Lord: let the Spirit lead and guide you.
You will be led to a place of rest and peace, too.
The devil seeks to steal your rest with his lies.
He wants to bind you with sinful ties.
Rest in the Lord: resist the devil; he will flee.
Rest in the Lord: it's what you hear, not what you see.
Rest in the Lord: you already know.
Seeking God's spiritual rest is the way to go.
Rest in the Lord: it can be a peaceful ride.
God's Word says He will never leave your side.
Rest in the Lord: it's a great place to be.
Rest in the Lord: there's where you'll find me!

Soaking Wet!

Soaking wet with God's spirit: it's like rain pouring down.
It will soak you up and turn your life around.
Getting soaking wet will change your dry attitude.
Soaking away the bad moods and depressing blues.
Getting soaking wet help deliver you from all that debt.
The swamping debt that constantly hangs around your neck.
Getting soaking wet helps soothe and renew your mind.
God's spirit will flow over you, like refreshing wine.
Getting soaking wet will touch and renew your soul.
Wow, you are feeling refreshed, powerful, and bold.
Get soaking wet: let it rain.
Soaking away your hurts and pain.
Getting soaking wet will saturate your weakened heart.
It will make it easier to be faithful and do your part.
Get soaking wet: the spirit of peace comes upon you.
It renews and brings the Holy Ghost's fire, too.
If you want to be soaking wet, say: "Lord, rain down on me!"
Pour, Pour, Pour: soaking in His supernatural spirit is the key!

Speak the Word!

II Corinthians 4:13: "We having the same spirit of faith, according as it is written, I believed and therefore have I spoken: we also believe, and therefore speak."
It is the Word of God that we seek!
Speak His Word, it will work miracles for you.
Speak the word and watch God do … it.
Faith will lead you to speak the word.
So much word, we have heard!
Speak the word,: wow, look at all that power!
Speak the word,: here comes the man of the hour!
Speak the word,: Satan must flee.
Speak the word,: it is the God in thee, he will see!
Speak the word,: tell that mountain to move, it must go.
Speak the word,: you can reap what you sow.
Speak the word: bow down and pray.
Speak the word: it will help you focus and stay.
Speak the word: it is your meat and bread.
Speak the word: let your spirit be fed.
Speak the word: get in the fight.
Speak the word: you will walk by faith and not by sight.
Speak the word faithfully through your test and mess.
Speak the word: God will bless and bless!
Speak the word: let it out.
Now, lift your hands and give a thankful and victory shout!

Submit and Resist!

Submit to God and resist the devil.
If you don't, he will take you to a whole nutty level.
Some Christians find it hard to submit.
They fuss about everything and throw all kinds of fits.
When it comes to the devil, they don't resist.
They realize too late the abundance and blessed life he has caused them to miss!
Submitting to God will bring you unsurpassed peace and rest.
Resist the devil and enjoy God's best!
Submit to God: He will not let you fall and let you down.
Resist the devil and know that what was lost is now found!
James 4:7 says, "Submit yourselves therefore to God. Resist the devil, and he will flee from you."
Submit to God and resist the devil is what we all need to do!
When we submit to God, He rules and reigns.
When we resist the devil, he goes insane.
Submit to God and resist the devil; do it today!
Now our God can bless you and have His way!

Take God out of the Box!

Take God out of the box; let Him out,.
And then he can work, blocking all of that doubt.
Take God out of that box; no need to fear.
He is ever-present, and always nearby.
Come on, let God out to rule and reign.
His Word is powerful; it will never change.
Take God out of the box; get out of His way.
Don't put Him on lockdown; release Him today!
Let Him out; He will never fit.
He is not a God to just sit and sit!
Take God out of that box; trust Him and wait.
For we serve a God that is always on time, never too late!
Take God out of that box; submit to His will.
Trust Him! Look up, and chill!

The Blessed Shall Remain Blessed.

Psalms 119:1: "Blessed are the undefiled in the way,"
They shall remain blessed every day.
Live a clean and undefiled life.
The blessings will overtake divisions and strife.
Psalms 119:2: "Blessed are they that keep His testimonies, and that seek him with the whole heart."
Those that seek God with their whole heart; they shall remain blessed when they walk by faith and do their part.
Psalms 119:3: "They also do no iniquity: they walk in his ways."
They shall remain blessed, trusting God, on Him they will depend.
Psalms 119:4: "Thou hast commanded us to keep thy precepts diligently."
We are commanded to keep his precepts (laws) diligently all the time.
If we don't, be prepared to suffer the punishment for the crime.
Psalms 1:2: "But his delight is in the law of the Lord; and in his law doth he meditates day and night."
The blessings come when we walk by faith and not by sight.
God does require us to be diligent, obey, and follow His commands.
When we do, he blesses what we faithfully touch with our hands.
Learn to walk God's way, there is nothing He will not do.
He will pour out His blessings, they will rain and fall all over you!

The Kingdom is in You!

The kingdom is in you; God put it there.
He wants you to feel His grace, mercy, and loving care.
Jesus is alive; He is living in you.
The Holy Ghost, our comforter, is in there, too.
He is the one who comforts us when we feel down.
And no matter where we go, He is always around.
The kingdom is full of God's blessings, flowing with milk and honey.
This kingdom cannot be ruled and bought with fake gold and money.
This kingdom is in you; you should take it everywhere you go.
It is the anointing of God, in case you didn't know!
The kingdom is in you; it is your strong tower.
This kingdom in you entitles you to God's Holy Ghost Power!
The kingdom is in you; strengthened by your faith.
The kingdom in you is God's amazing grace.
The kingdom is in you; touch your anointed hand to your heart.
The kingdom in you says, "DO YOUR PART!"
When all is said and done.
The kingdom in you has already won!

"The Lord is my Shepherd" (Psalms 23)

"The Lord is my shepherd; I shall not want."
When my God says, "Don't worry," I don't!
"He maketh me lie down in green pastures, He leadeth me."
Besides his still waters is where I long to be!
"He restoreth my soul."
His peace unfolds!
"Yea, though I walk through the valley of the shadow of death,
I will not fear."
For His words of courage, I hold dear!
"Thy rod and thy staff, they comfort me."
Your goodness is all I can see!
"Thou preparest a table before me in the presence of
my enemies,
Thou anointest my head with oil."
My God erases all the pain, hurt, and turmoil!
"Surely goodness and mercy shall follow me all the days
of my life."
By His Word, I will have a life full of blessings without
the strife!
Now this last line, I quote loudly to all listening devils:
"And I will dwell in the house of the Lord forever."

Trust God.

Trust God: "He is not a man that He should lie."
He is the one who gives us mighty wings to fly
above and beyond our tests and trials:
to help us to touch the hem of his garment even in the midst
of a crowd!
Trust God: Wait on Him; He will show up on the scene.
Trust God: upon his shoulders, you can lean!
Trust God: meditate on His Word day and night.
He will help you win; it is a fixed fight!
Trust in God: don't always look for miracles and signs.
Just trust God every day and every time!
Trust God: Go ahead, you can boast
of this awesome God who filled you with His Holy Ghost!
Trust God: Walk by faith in all that you do.
Trust God: He will do the impossible things for you!
Trust God: He is the truth, our shining light.
Trust God: He is awesome, wonderful and just right!

The Word of God!

Thew Word of God speaks out today.
The Word of God guides and leads the way.
The Word of God is alive.
The Word of God puts pep in your stride.
The Word of God will humble you and make you cry.
The Word of God will not lie.
The Word of God will make you bold.
The Word of God cries out for souls.
The Word of God calls all to come in.
The Word of God washes you clean of all sins.
The Word of God will lift you up.
The Word of God will fill and overflow your cup.
The Word of God wants you to live.
The Word of God knows how you feel.
The Word of God is healing to your bones.
The Word of God offers you the key to His heavenly home.
The Word of God commands you to live right.
The Word of God gives you victory in every battle or fight.
The Word of God can only be fulfilled
when you accept Jesus Christ as your savior and obey His will.
The Word of God says: don't harden your heart when God
calls out to you!
The Word of God says: just make up your mind and
choose Him, too!

When You Can't, God Can!

When you can't, God can! He is your power.
He is your strength and your strong tower.
When you can't, God can! He will lift you up.
He is the only one who can fill your anointed cup.
When you can't, God can! It is His time.
He is your Heavenly father; He is your lifeline.
When you can't, God can! He is real.
Give all your pains to Him, He will heal!
When you can't, God can! He washes away all sin stains,
sending them forever down the drain.
When you can't, God can! On Him, you need to depend.
Open your heart and let Him in!
When you can't, God can! He is your bread.
Take it, eat it, and be fed.
When you can't, God can! Be patient and wait.
Watch out; don't take Satan's bait.
When you can't, God can! Be faithful through every test.
God is your victory; He will show up and bring you out of
your troubles and mess.
When you can't, God can! All needs are met.
What you sow, you will reap and get.
When you can't, God can! Always pray!
When you can't, God can! He will lead and guide you all the
way every day!

Your Miracle Comes Out of Your Mess.

So, you have some trials and a few tests,
Losing sleep and getting no rest.
Bills keep piling up!
You are praying faithfully, "Lord, fill my cup!"
Pain attacking your body, so weak,
but the Lord's help you can continue to seek.
The man of God preaching about trials and tests.
And then he says, "Your miracle comes out of your mess!"
Could this be true?
Was this message just for you?
It was a wakeup call, opening your tired eyes.
His words have broken through the devil's lies.
He continues to preach and says, "Get ready for God's best!
Your miracle comes out of your mess!"
And as the man of God is praying,
I meditate on what he was saying.
Trials, troubles, mountains, storms, and tests,
We're preparing me for a miracle to come out of my mess!

HIS NAME IS JESUS

Crucify that Flesh.

Crucify that flesh, it wants to rule and reign.
But we know there is only one ruler: Jesus is His name.
Jesus went to the cross, but not to save the flesh.
Watch out, this stuff will keep you in a mess.
Crucify that flesh; it will try to control you.
Flesh will tell your mind and soul what to do.
Crucify that flesh; there is nothing good in it.
Crucify that flesh; it seeks to lead you into a fiery pit.
Crucify that flesh; don't let it lead you astray.
You need to crucify that flesh every day.
Crucify that flesh; it will lead you back into sin.
Walk by faith; you can beat it and win.
Crucify that flesh; don't let it steal your holy light.
Crucify that flesh; this takes a faith fight.
Crucify that flesh; crucify it through every test.
Crucify that flesh; don't let it steal God's best.
Galatians 5:16: "This I say then, walk in the Spirit, and ye shall not
fulfill the lust of the flesh."
Walk in the spirit and you will be blessed!

Death to Self; Let Christ Live in You.

The flesh wants you to have it way.
It seeks to rule and reign every day.
The flesh will tie you up in a mess.
And cause you to miss God's best.
Death to self; crucify that flesh.
Live in the Spirit; receive God's rest.
The flesh will lead you astray.
And, eventually, you will have to pay.
The price can be extremely high.
Don't let the flesh rule; don't buy the lie.
Death to self; let Christ live in you.
He will bless everything that you do.
Death to self; let God's spirit in.
Death to self; remember, we win!

Do You Know Jesus?

Do you know Jesus? Haven't you heard?
You can read about Him in the Bible, God's holy Word.
Do you know Jesus? He gave his life as a living sacrifice.
He went to the cross and paid the heavenly price.
Do you know Jesus? He sits on the right hand of God above.
He is our advocate, a mediator of God's love.
Do you know Jesus? On Him, you can depend.
He is a true and faithful friend.
Do you know Jesus? I hope he knows you.
Then he will be present in your heart and present in all that you do.
Do you know Jesus? He is the way, the truth, and the life.
Knowing him, you can live free of divisions and strife.
Do you know Jesus? He should be the reason
that we celebrate Him throughout all seasons.
Do you know Jesus? He teaches us to live a life of love and giving.
He walks through with his words so that we can enjoy a life of good living.
Do you know Jesus? Call on Him during your trials and tests.
Be thankful when He blesses you with His peace and rest.
Do you know Jesus? I hope that you do. If not, just open up your heart and confess.
Yes, I want to know Jesus and receive him as my Savior, then I, too, can have his best!

Get Addicted to Jesus.

I don't know how it feels to get high.
I don't know how it feels to touch the sky.
They say being addicted to anything is really bad.
It can only bring you heartache and make you sad.
But there is one addiction that is good for you.
Get addicted to Jesus; it's what you need to do.
Get addicted to Jesus: it's a Holy Ghost High.
He will give you the anointed power to fly…over all obstacles.
Get addicted to Jesus; this kind of high won't mess you up.
It will make you say again and again: "Lord, fill my cup."
Get addicted to Jesus; you won't ever come down.
You will float above every situation; there is joy to be found!
Get addicted to Jesus; this the good stuff.
He will help you when times get rough.
Get addicted to Jesus; it's a high that can't be beat.
It will put praise in your heart and dance in your feet.
Get addicted to Jesus; this high is free.
I got addicted to Jesus: wow, look at me!
Get addicted to Jesus; it's the only way to go.
Get addicted to Jesus and let it flow!

Got Jesus?

Got Jesus? Well, you have more than enough
to press through when times are tough.
Got Jesus? He is the one who sets us free.
He can do it for you because he did it for me.
Got Jesus? You have all that you need.
He will prune your life, pull up those weeds.
Got Jesus? You got the best.
He will be with you through every test.
Got Jesus? You got your peace!
Got Jesus? Let all other voices cease.
Got Jesus? Draw close to Him. Hold him tight.
Got Jesus? Hallelujah! You finally got it right.

His Name is Jesus: A Skit.

He was born, he lived.
He came to obey and do the Father's will.
His name is Jesus.

He turned water into wine.
He gave sight to the blind.
He fed five thousand with five fish and a loaf of bread.
He raised Lazarus from the dead.
His name is Jesus.

He preached, "I came to do the Father's will."
He spoke to the wind, "Peace, be still."
His name is Jesus.

He cast out demons; the dumb talked.
He gave strength to crippled legs and they walked!
His name is Jesus.

He taught the disciples to pray.
And we still say "The Lord's Prayer" today.
His name is Jesus.

The devil came to tempt him in the wilderness.
For forty days, he had no food or rest.
Now when it was all said and done,
Jesus whipped him with His Word and won.
His name is Jesus.

Jesus walked the Earth, never making a scene.
Even though those Pharisees were acting so mean.

They were always lurking around, seeking to catch
Him in a lie;
always asking Him to show them and explain why.
Why should they believe what he was saying?
They were spending too much time on their false praying.
His name is Jesus.
Jesus' work on this Earth came to an end.
It was now time to go to the cross for forgiveness of our sins.
His name is Jesus.

Jesus prayed until the time came.
Judas greeted him with a kiss, Peter went insane.
He cut off the man's ear.
He was swinging his sword in anger and fear.
After healing the man's ear, Jesus had nothing more to say.
The soldiers grabbed him, and the disciples ran away.
His name is Jesus.
The blood- thirsty crowd was screaming, "Crucify, crucify;"
the scene was set.
It was a sacrifice no one would ever forget.
Jesus died on the cross.
He had fulfilled his Father's will, giving his life for the lost.
His name is Jesus.

Those Pharisees thought they had won the last round.
But God was just getting ready to throw down.
Three hours, there was darkness, no light, and then:
the Earth shook, tombs opened; Godly men and women
came to life!
It was a marvelous sight!
His name is Jesus.

One, two, three days, the stone was rolled away, and Jesus walked out!
All lost souls had reason to shout!
He told the disciples to go on the highways and streets.
He told Peter, "Feed my sheep."
His name is Jesus.
He lived; he died for you and me.
He rose up to set us free.
His name is Jesus!

I Am the Door!

I am the door: come, enter it.
I am here to save and forgive your sins.
I am the door: come, is it healing you seek?
I will heal your body and soul, give you strength when you are weak.
I am the door: knock, this door with always be open for you.
The willing and obedient will receive my blessing dew.
I am the door: walk in, seek my face.
I will rain down my mercy and grace.
I am the door: I will never lock you out.
You have the keys; now erase all your doubts.
I am the door: are you seeking some release?
The door is open, come and receive my peace.
I am the door: that old devil is like roaring lion seeking to destroy.
Enter in; I will give you unsurpassed peace and fullness of joy.
I am the door; come on in, be thou blessed.
Seek me now; I will quench your thirst.
I am the door: Jesus is my name.
Come on in, let it rain!

Jesus: He is Everything We Need!

Luke 2:11: "For unto you is born this day into the city of David a savior, which is Christ the Lord."
Jesus, we thank you for your salvation cord.
Acts 9:20: "And straightway he preached Christ in the synagogues, that he is the son of God."
Jesus, the holy son of God. He is our faithful rod.
1st Peter 5:4: "And when the Chief Shepherd shall appear; ye shall receive a crown of glory that fades not away."
Jesus, our shepherd, watches over his sheep (us) every day.
1st John 2:1: "My little children, these things I write unto you, that ye sin not. And if any man sin, we have an advocate with our Father/Jesus Christ righteous."
He is our advocate; He goes before the Father and says, "I stand in the gap; they are worth the price."
John 6:51: "I am the living bread which came down from Heaven: If any man eats of this bread, he shall live forever: and the bread that I will give is my flesh, which I will give for the life of the world."
Jesus, our living bread: He is more precious than diamonds and pearls.
John 14:6: "Jesus saith unto him, I am the way, the truth and the life: no man cometh unto the father but by me."
Jesus: He is our way, our truth, and our life; He is the only one that brings us to the Father and that's the way it's going to be.
1st Timothy 2 5:6: "For there is one God, and one mediator between God and men, the man Christ Jesus, who gave himself a ransom for all, to be testified in due time."
Yes, He is the mediator who helps our holy heart to always chime.
Hebrews 12:2: "Looking unto Jesus the author and finisher of our faith."

The author and finisher of our faith leads and keeps us safe. Isaiah 9:6: "For unto us a child is born, unto us a son is given; and the government shall be upon his shoulder: and his name shall be called Wonderful, Counsellor, The mighty God, The everlasting Father, The Prince of Peace."

Jesus is everything we need; speak His name and all other divisions, strives, and voices will cease!

Jesus, I Will Never Forget.

Jesus, the Lord of my life, I will never forget,
when you and I first met.
I had no knowledge of you, never prayed;
and so, I approached the altar, so afraid.
Yet, I somehow knew I would not leave the same.
And I could finally say goodbye to all the shame.
I was now being released from my jail.
You did that for me with a very painful nail.
Jesus, I will never forget, how you gave and gave
so that your blood could save and save.
I stood crying joyful tears,
refreshed and clean of all my fears.
Jesus, I will never forget such love for me.
Yes, you set this captive free.
He wiped away every scarlet stain
and healed me of so much pain.
Jesus, I will never forget. You're always in my heart.
What a great place to start!
Jesus, I will never forget. You touched my soul
I belong to Him, a part of His sheepfold.
Jesus, I will never forget. I will run this race
until the day I meet you face to face.

Jesus Makes Life Better!

Walk by faith; never say "never."
Jesus makes life better and better!
Don't be locked down and entangled in the cares of life.
Jesus makes life better; no need to live a life full of strife.
Break out; renew your mind and heart.
Let Jesus make life better and give you a new start.
Jesus said, "If any man will come after me, let him deny himself,
take up his cross and follow me."
Jesus makes life better when you walk by faith, not by what you see.
Matthew 16:26: "For what is man profited, if he gains the whole world,
and lose his own soul?"
Jesus makes life better: walk by faith, sow that seed and receive your
hundred-fold.
Pursue and chase after Jesus every day.
Jesus makes life better and better when you do it His way.
Remember, it is God who gives us power to get wealth and adds no
sorrow.
Jesus makes life better; now you can lend not borrow.
Don't get weary; trust and believe for God's best.
Jesus makes life better, and along comes peace and rest.
Keep Jesus first, let him be the head.
Jesus makes life better; he is alive not dead.
Jesus makes your life better and better!
Make Him Lord and never say "never" again.

Jesus: Our Hope is in You.

Lamentations 3:24: "The Lord is my portion, saith my soul; therefore, will I hope in him."
Jesus, our hope is in you; you are our branch and limb.
Psalms 31:24: "Be of good courage, and he shall strengthen your heart, all ye hope in the Lord."
Jesus, our hope is in you; the Word of God is our sword.
Acts 2:26: "Therefore did my heart rejoice, and my tongue was glad; moreover, also my flesh shall rest in hope."
Jesus, our hope is in you; it's our life-saving rope.
Psalms 33:22: "Let thy mercy, O Lord, be upon us, according as we hope in thee."
Jesus, our hope is in you; thanks for setting us free.
Romans 12:12: "Rejoicing in hope; patient in tribulations; continuing instant in prayer."
Jesus is our hope; we know He is always there.
1st Timothy 1:1: "Paul, an apostle of Jesus Christ by the commandment of God our savior, and Lord Jesus Christ which is our hope;"
Jesus, our hope is in you; bringing liberty and deliverance from bondage and yokes.
1st John 3:3: "And every man that hath his hope in him purifieth himself, even as pure."
Jesus, our hope is in you; He alone helps us endure.
Titus 1:2: "In hope of eternal life, which God, that cannot lie, promised before the world began;"
Jesus, our hope is in you; for eternal life, we will faithfully stand!
Psalms 71:14: "But I will hope continually and will yet praise thee more and more."
Jesus, our hope is in you; we will mount up as wings of eagles and soar!

Jesus, Our Savior.

1st John 4:14: "And we have seen and do testify that the father sent the son
to be the savior of the world."
He saved us, and now to Him, we are more precious than diamonds or pearls.
Luke 2:11: "For unto you is born this day in the city of David a savior, which is Christ the Lord."
He is our savior, whom we love, worship, and truly adore.
1st Timothy 4:10: "For therefore we both labor and suffer reproach, because we trust in the living God, who is the savior of all men specifically those that believe."
Jesus, our savior: His gift of salvation we gladly receive.
2 Peter 3:18: "But grow in grace, and in the knowledge of our Lord and Savior Jesus Christ.
To him be glory both now and forever. Amen."
Luke 1:47: "And my spirit hath rejoiced in God my savior."
Jesus, our savior: we thank Him for his blessed favor.
Jude 1:25: "To the only wise God our savior, be glory and majesty, dominion, and power, both now and ever. Amen."
Jesus, our savior: with Him, we conquer all and win.

Jesus Said it: That's Enough.

The Bible is full of the powerful words Jesus said.
Romans 10:9: "That if you confess with your mouth, 'Jesus is Lord,' and believe in
your heart that God raised him from the dead, you will be saved."
Jesus said it; that's enough for me.
We need to focus on his words, not what we see.
Luke 11:9: "So I say unto you; ask and it will be given to you; seek and
you will find; knock and the door will be opened to you."
Jesus said it; that's enough, believe it, that's all you need to do.
John 15:12: "My command is this: Love each other as I have loved you."
Jesus said it; that's enough, love your way through.
Romans 8:37: "No, in all things we are more than conquerors through
him who loved us."
Jesus said it; that's enough. In Him, you can put your trust.
Philippians 4:19: "And my God will supply all your needs according to
his riches and glory in Christ Jesus." He will meet that need.
Jesus said it; that's enough. Now, plant those seeds.
Mark 14:38: "Watch and pray so that you will not fall into temptation:
The spirit is willing, but the flesh is weak."
Jesus said it; that's enough. Pray, and your soul He will keep.
Psalm 71:8: "My mouth is filled with your praise, declaring your splendor all day long."
Jesus said it; that's enough. He is the only one who can make right every
wrong.

Jesus!

J is for Jesus: the savior who saved me.
The one who said love is the key.
E is for eternity: He lives forever.
And one day, we will be in eternity together.
S is for salvation: His free gift of love
our heavenly father offers from above.
U is for us: we are the ones He calls.
He wants us to break and tear down every wall.
S is for souls: giving their lives to Him every day.
He will lead and guide them all the way.

Leaning on Jesus.

Lean on Jesus when times get rough.
Lean on Jesus; He will strengthen you, make you tough.
Lean on Jesus when you are sick.
Lean on Jesus when you lose your kick.
Lean on Jesus; say goodbye to stress.
Lean on Jesus, He will give you much needed rest.
Lean on Jesus; get your peace.
It is His guaranteed lifeline lease.
Lean on Jesus, all is well.
Don't walk around, a broken and empty shell.
Lean on Jesus, the devil must flee.
Now you can be like the tree
that is planted by the river, look at the overflow.
Lean on Jesus, your fruits will ripen and grow.
Lean on Jesus; he won't move.
Trust him; you have nothing to lose.
Lean on Jesus; every heart he will mend.
Lean on Jesus; on Him you can depend.
Lean on Jesus; "he is not a man that he should lie."
Lean on Jesus; on him you can rely.
Lean on Jesus; trust and believe.
Leaning on Jesus, you just opened the door to receive.

Stand for Christ.

Stand for Christ; stand strong, don't bow to the devil.
Choose to stand for Christ and for God to move you to a whole new level.
Stand for Christ; allow God to make a deposit in us.
Stand for Christ; in Him we do put our trust.
Stand for Christ; let Him live richly in you.
It's not only what you say, but the action you do.
Stand for Christ; for the devil seeks to put you in a squeeze.
Stand for Christ; walk by faith and trust God: He will lead.
Stand for Christ; He is there during your fight.
He will guide you through the darkness into a marvelous light.
Stand for Christ; there will be haters.
Be strong; He who is in you, is greater.
Stand for Christ; don't be deceived.
What you say is what you will receive.
Stand for Christ; speak to that mountain, it has got move.
Standing for Christ and walking by faith are mighty tools.
Stand for Christ; sometimes we may stumble
but the greater one, God, never sleeps nor slumbers.
Stand for Christ; you have made the right choice.
Stand for Christ; give Him praise and rejoice.
Stand for Christ; don't just have a form of godliness, denying His power.
Choose to stand for Christ this very hour!

They Just Don't Know.

Jesus is the way: follow Him, get up and go.
But too many are saying, "I just don't know."
So many souls sitting on the pew.
The pleasures of this world are blocking their view.
Every day, they are taking Satan's bait.
They don't know that it's too late.
God is waiting, He is ready to save.
They just don't know the road has been paved.
He is the only one that can take away the shame.
His healing touch will heal the pain.
They just don't know: there is no reason to be afraid.
The price has already been paid.
They just don't know; Jesus is the key.
Break loose from those chains, you are free!
I just don't know what else to say,
but: "Come to Jesus, come today!"

What a Price He Paid!

We were sinful, filthy as dirty rags.
We deserved death and a toe tag.
Leaving this world, we were on our way to Hell,
never to be released from our eternal cell.
But, one day, He came: our savior, our king.
He stepped in and forever changed the scene.
He spoke, "I take every sin upon me."
Release them, set the captives free."
What a price he paid!
Death and fear have no more power over us.
Eternal life waits: no more ashes to ashes and dust to dust.
We are covered by His blood and His love.
Yes, we have a home in heaven above.
What a price he paid!
He healed all sickness, diseases: he took it all.
All we have to do is call.
He is the mighty man of the hour.
He restores all with his anointing power.
No more loss, poverty, and lack;
Jesus is our weapon of attack.
What a price he paid!

SALVATION

Priceless.

"For God so loved the world that He gave his only begotten son to die on the cross."
His sacrifice frees us from sin and gives salvation to all that are lost.
It is a gift: free, at no cost.
When it comes to God's love for us, it is priceless.

There is no charge for his peace, love, and joy.
He freely gives to all who asks.
The God we serve is real; He wears no mask.
He doesn't need your money, stocks, bonds, or gold.
His story of love and sacrifice has already been told.
Don't be fooled by religion and tradition.
God's love for us is priceless.

The gift of salvation: priceless. It is not for sale.
The Holy Spirit: priceless. Ask Simon, he tried to buy it.
The fruits of the spirit: priceless. God wants your tree to be full.
Spiritual gifts: priceless. God divides them to every man as He wills.
Prosperity: priceless. There is no limit you can put on God's goodness.
Divine healing: priceless. You can't find this in a drugstore.
Eternal life: priceless And they believed that they had struck it rich when they discovered the so-called fountain of youth.

No commercials, no gimmicks, no luck of the draw.
Look for everything you need in God's covenant law.
And why is it priceless?

"Because God so loved the world that he gave his only begotten son, that whosoever believeth in him should not perish but have everlasting life." John 3:16

How Can I Hear You?

Clutter, worries, sickness clouds my mind.
Blocking my ears, no peace can I find.
Conditions, tests, and turmoil, I try to escape;
and truly, I've had about all I can take.
What to do with all this mess?
Feeling alone, and doubtful, I must confess.
How can I hear what you are saying?
Oh, don't even talk about fasting and praying.
That old devil using every trick to bring me down.
Here I stand, not even making a sound.
How can I hear you with so much going on?
I ask myself, "Do you belong?"
How can I hear, less more see when the one in the way is *me*!
How can I hear you? Spirit, unstop my ears!
Quench the fiery darts, bind my fears!
How can I hear? I need to know.
'Cause I am ready for the blessings to flow!
How can I hear? Here's the key;
Recognize that in Christ, you are free!
Trust Him, Love Him, every day of the year!
I ask you now, "Can you hear?"

Not only Forgiven, but Forgotten.

Psalm 103:3 says, "Who forgiveth all thine iniquities." He heals all pain.
He washes away our sins, forgotten, down the drain.
Not only forgiven, but forgotten, too.
It is a gift of His never-ending love for you.
The past is the past; you need to let it go.
Jesus' blood washes you clean and makes you whiter than snow.
Not only forgiven, but forgotten: your sins are cast into the sea.
He will do it for you; He did it for me.
Not only forgiven, but forgotten; He remembers them no more.
Stop looking back: God has closed that door.
Not only forgiven, but forgotten: living sin-free.
If you want this kind of life, accepting Jesus is the key.

Break it Down.

Matthew 4:17 says, "Repent: for the kingdom of heaven is at hand."
This is Jesus' cry to every sinner born in this land.
So much is going on and going down.
Yet God is loving and saying, "Seek you the Lord while he may be found,
call upon him while he is near."
Let me break it down for you, and
then you can decide what to do:
Jesus went to the cross and not in vain;
He did it so that you and I reign
victorious, strong, prosperous, healed, and free.
He offers his gift of salvation, no fee.
Let me break it down to those who haven't found our wonderful savior;
He is the one who doesn't condemn us with our past and sinful behavior.
Let me break it down, this is what it is all about:
Sinners are dying every day; time is running out.
Some people don't think that they need God because their days
are prosperous and sunny.
Remember that the Bible says: "You can't serve God and money."
Let me break it down and show you the deal:
If God is not first in your life, then you are out of His will.
God is offering his salvation, free of charge.
There is no deposit or interest required for this card.
Take the first step, repent, and accept Jesus right away.
Do it now and make His day!

Salvation is for All.

Listen to God, hear, and answer His call!
Speak His word, for salvation is for all!
Salvation is for all: ask for forgiveness and repent.
There is no price, salvation is not for rent.
Our God is offering His salvation to all.
Accept Jesus, respond to and accept His call.
Salvation will help to build you up,
for God will answer you and fill your cup!
Salvation is for all: walk by faith and not by sight.
Accept Jesus, He will give you victory in every fight.
Salvation is for all, receive Jesus as your savior; He is with you always!
He will lead and guide you every day.
Jesus hears you when you bow and pray.
Salvation is for all, listen and hear what God has to say!
Salvation is for all, no need to fear.
When you answer His call, Jesus is always here and near.
Salvation is for all: now is the time to answer His call!
He will help you stand back up when you stumble and fall.
Open your eyes and ears, see and hear that the devil is a liar!
He is not your healer nor your supplier.
Salvation is for all: God calls the sinners to repentance, and the sick.
These are the ones that God calls you to seek and pick.
Salvation is for all!
Again, hear Him and accept His call!

Now Is the Time for Salvation.

II Corinthians 6:2 says, "…behold now is the accepted time; behold,
now is the day of salvation."
It is time to come off our procrastination vacation.
God is reaching out to us every day.
Will you open your heart and receive the words He has to say?
Time is always slipping by, fading fast.
Don't get stuck and lost in your past.
Proverbs 27:1 says, "Boast not thyself of tomorrow; for thou knowest
not what a day may bring forth."
You have heard that tomorrow isn't promised to us
and that one day we will return to dust.
Please don't leave this world the way you came in.
Jesus offers salvation and deliverance from sin.
Don't put off having a relationship with God today.
Come to Him and let the Holy Spirit have His way.
It's time to bring an end to heartache and strife.
Accept Jesus now and start a new life.
God will always be there, and He will bless
you with his love, peace, joy, prosperity, and eternal rest.

Repent, God Wants You To.

When I think of repentance, I think of what John the Baptist had to say.
We still read about those powerful words today.
Matthew 3:1-2: "In those days came John the Baptist, preaching in the
wilderness of Judea, and saying, Repent ye; for the kingdom of heaven
is at hand."
This is a message that we can easily understand.
Repentance means to feel Godly sorrow, to turn away from sin.
Listen to John; he knew what it took to win.
Come to Jesus, while he can be found.
He is ever-present and always around.
Sin draws us away from God and His will.
Sin will give the devil room to steal and kill.
Romans 6:23: "For the wages of sin is death.
But the gift of God is eternal life through Jesus Christ, our Lord."
Repent: give God the praise and glory.
Let him put a happy ending to your story.
Jesus paid the price and the cost.
He died that none should perish and be lost.
Don't leave this earth the way you came in.
Let Jesus save you and free you from sin.
Repent, don't waste your precious time.
God is coming; there will be no warnings or signs.
Will you be ready? I ask you again, will you be ready?
Isaiah 55:6-7: "Seek ye the Lord while he may be found, call ye upon
him while he is near: Let the wicked forsake his way, and the

unrighteous man his thoughts and let him return unto the Lord, and He
will have mercy; and to our God, for he will abundantly pardon."

Salvation: Do you Accept this Free Gift?

Salvation is a free gift offered to everyone.
Do you accept this gift and what Jesus has done?
Salvation is a free gift for all who are lost.
Jesus gave it to us when he went to the cross.
Salvation: accept Jesus, that's all you have to do.
Behold, old things pass away; all things become new.
Salvation: do you accept this free gift?
It will clean you from all of your dirty sins and filth.
Salvation is a free gift, you have the choice to say yes or no.
Make the right one and Jesus will lead you down the path to go.
He is the salvation that we need.
Accept Him, and he will pull up and burn all those sinful weeds.
Salvation: do you accept this free gift that cleanses you from lustful
sins?
Now you have the savior to fight every battle and help you win!
Salvation: do you accept this free gift? It is offered to all who will come.
It is His gift to all, not just some.
Salvation: do you accept this free gift? His name is Jesus.
He waits patiently for you through every season.

Salvation, God's Gift to You.

If I were to take your Bible and look up Romans 10:9,
it would show us the way to salvation every time.
For no better words have been said,
nor more beautiful words ever read.
These words are God's salvation plan for man.
Reach out and trust Him, follow his commands.
Romans 10:9: "That if thou shalt confess with thy mouth the Lord Jesus,
and shalt believe in thine heart that God hath raised him from the dead,
and shalt be saved."
And so, we can see, the road has been paved.
No debris, garbage, past or present sin;
no, nothing can stop you from making it in.
Let the true story be told.
Jesus came not to judge, but to save your soul.
While we were sinners, Jesus died that we might have eternal life.
God loved us so much that he gave his only begotten son as the sacrificial price.
God has given us a second chance to get this right.
He delivered us from the kingdom of darkness and brought us into the kingdom of His marvelous light.
God is the answer; He will quench our thirst.
Never forget that God loved us first.
Jesus shed his blood, he died and rose again.
Accept his salvation, defeat sin and win.

Saved is the Way.

Saved is the way.
Jesus is still saving today.
Saved is the way: it cleanses your soul.
This is something I read and know.
Saved is the way: it sets us free.
Remember our savior, Jesus, hung on that tree.
Saved is the way: you must do your part.
Accept his salvation and Him into your heart.
Saved is the way: it is our much-needed light.
Jesus saves us and makes everything right.
Saved is the way: it will open blinded eyes.
He is merciful and faithful to hear our cries.
Saved is the way: Jesus guides our every step.
He is always leading us and giving us much needed help.
Saved is the way: Jesus went to the cross for us all.
Don't hang up on Him, accept his call.
Saved is the way: go ahead and confess.
Being saved, cleaned, righteous and loved: what a way to be blessed!

Say What You Believe; Believe What You Say.

Jesus went to the cross to save the lost.
It didn't matter to Him what it cost.
It was His to give, He gave His life.
He is our savior; He paid the price.
Say what you believe; believe what you say.
Jesus is still saving the lost every day.
We have an enemy who came to kill, steal, and destroy.
Say what you believe; believe what you say; Jesus is our peace, He is our
joy.
He came that we might be free and live.
He came to redeem, restore, and heal.
Say what you believe; believe what you say.
Jesus will lead and guide you all the way.
He will give you victory in everything that you do.
His spirit will live and abide in you.
Give Jesus a chance, give him a try.
He will give you wings like eagles; you will fly!
Say what you believe; believe what you say.
Say and believe, do it today.

Seven Steps to Salvation.

Realize that you have sinned.
A sinner can never win.

Truly repent of your sins, turn away.
Listen to what the Word of God has to say.

Confess your sins; He will forgive.
It is His purpose for you to be saved and live.

Forsake your sins: let them go.
Don't harden your heart and tell Him no.

Ask forgiveness for your sins; let God wash you clean.
He wants you saved and on His Holy Ghost team.

Consecrate your entire life to Christ; let your light shine.
Feel the joy when you hear Jesus say, "That one is mine."

Believe that Jesus saves you by his grace.
Without His mercy, you can't win this race.

Will You be Ready?

A trumpet sounds: the time is here.
Jesus has come, no need to fear.
He has come to take us home,
where we will never be alone.
But now that is the time.
An important question comes to mind:
will you be ready
when our master breaks the sky?
Will you be there to hear his joyful cry?
He is not coming by bus, train, or ship.
Will you be ready to make this trip?
He is coming back for those who have been
washed in the blood and changed.
He won't care about rank or the title in your name.
He will be looking for the ones who walked by faith,
not by sight.
He is coming for those who didn't faint nor give up the fight.
Will you be ready when Jesus comes for his bride?
There will be no hookups or free rides.
So, take a good, long look at your life:
make sure you won't be left behind and surprised.
When Jesus comes back, and He will,
Let us be full of truth and let us be real.
Will you be ready?

FAITH

Faith.

Hebrews 11: 1 says, "Faith is the substance of things hoped for, the evidence of things not seen."
Faith and the Holy Spirit make an awesome team!
When you have faith in God, there will be a change in your behavior.
You will faithfully accept Jesus as your Lord and Savior!
True faith leads you to hear His Word and do it.
True faith in God accepts His Word that will raise you from the devil's dark pit.
Romans 10:17 says, "So then faith cometh by hearing and hearing the word of God."
God gives each of us a measure of faith that we must grow: it takes a teachable spirit and a desire to know.
"Without faith, it is impossible to please God." Don't even try.
It is His faith-filled children who are the apple of his eye!
Let us remember and keep James 2:20 in our heads:
"Faith without works is dead."

Fight to Win.

I give up; I am tired; I just can't take it.
I am about to go off and pitch a fit.
I don't know what I need to do.
My Lord, it is so hard to obey and live for you.
What is going on in your head?
Let the Holy Spirit live and your flesh stay dead!
Don't you know that you must fight to win?
Fight every urge that wants to lead you back to your life of sin.
Fight to win; the battle has already been won.
Look and see what our mighty God has done!
Fight to win; you must be wise,
for the devil comes in every disguise.
Fight to win; God requires it of you.
Fight to win, and the winner will come through.
Fight to win; walk by faith, not by sight.
Come on, we win! Claim the fight of faith!

Get a Grip!

Get a grip; hold on tight.
God's Word will renew your strength for your fight.
Get a grip; don't lose your hope.
Grab onto faith: it is your life's rope.
Times can be hard and take a toll.
Life can take you down some bumpy roads.
Get a grip; you must know:
God is with us wherever we go.
Get a grip; we conquer in Jesus' name.
With His love, there is no shame.
Remember that we can have whatsoever we say.
Get a grip: let the God in you have His way!

Standing on Your Faith.

Stand on your faith; don't focus on what the devil is doing.
Look at God; He is the one you need to be pursuing.
Standing on faith: let go of that fear.
You see, Satan comes to steal your faith: listen, and hear.
Faith must say, speak, and do.
Standing on faith is left up to you.
When we stand faithful and strong,
God will be faithful to right every wrong.
Faith in God will not fail.
We keep standing; our faith is not for sale.
When we stand on faith, God always shows up on the scene.
He brings His Holy Ghost power: what a team!
Standing on faith: you need to chew and eat this meat.
It is your choice: choose victory, not defeat!
Standing on faith is all about who you believe.
Standing on faith: open your hands and get ready to receive!
You must heed His Word: walk by faith, not by sight!
Standing on faith: knowing that God has already won
the fight!

When Faith Shows Up.

Hebrews 11:1: "Now faith is the substance of things hoped for, the evidence of things not seen."
When faith shows up, get ready to be redeemed.
II Corinthians 5:7: "For we walk by faith, not by sight."
When faith shows up, get ready to win the fight.
Mark 9:23: "Everything is possible for him who believes."
When faith shows up, open your hands and receive.
Luke 7:50: "Jesus said to the woman, your faith has saved you; go in peace."
When faith shows up, all turmoil must cease.
John 14:14: "If ye shall ask anything in my name, I will do it."
When faith shows up, God is ready to commit.
Luke 1:37: "For with God nothing is impossible." He can turn it around.
When faith shows up, you don't have to fear that roaring lion. (Satan)
James 2:17: "Even so faith, if it hath not works, is dead, being alone."
When faith shows up, your actions will set the best tone.
Mark 11:22: "And Jesus answered saith unto them, Have faith in God." You need to trust Him today!
When faith shows up, you can have whatsoever you say!

The Power of Faith.

Romans 10:17: "So then faith cometh by hearing, and hearing by
the word of God"
The power of faith comes by hearing the word.
A faith that works by what you received and heard.
Hebrews 11:6: "But without faith, it is impossible to please him."
The power of faith: seek it, don't let it go dim.
Hebrews 11:1: "Now faith is the substance of things hoped for, the
Evidence of things not seen."
The power of faith makes you and God a powerful team.
2nd Corinthians 5:7: "For we walk by faith, not by sight."
The power of faith is worth the fight.
1st Corinthians 16:13: "Be on your guard, stand firm; be men of courage;
Be strong."
The power of faith will renew and strengthen your weary bones.
1st Corinthians 2:5: "So that your faith not rest on men's wisdom, but on
God's power."
The power of faith can reign upon us this very hour.
Galatians 5:5: "But by faith we eagerly await through the spirit,
The righteous for which we hope."
The power of faith keeps us afloat.
Ephesians 6:16: "Above all, taking the shield of faith, wherewith ye shall
Be able to quench all the fiery darts of the wicked."
The power of faith is your one-way ticket.

1st John 5:4: "For whatsoever is born of God overcometh the world; and
This is victory that overcometh the world, even our faith."
The power of faith ensures that we feel protected and safe.
The power of faith is something we all need. It opens the doors to all who believe.
The power of faith can save and set free. It is here for you and me to receive!

Choose Not to Faint!

Tests and trials will cause you to faint.
You focus on that mountain and say, "I can't."
Choose not to faint; keep pressing.
It is a faith-walk that keeps God blessing.
Choose not to faint; walk in God's strength.
It is a faith-walk, not about what you think.
Get on the rock, faint not.
Everything you need, God's got.
Choose not to faint; give the devil no room.
He just wants to bring you gloom and doom.
Choose not to faint; troubles will come your way.
Be steadfast, unmovable: God hears you when you pray.
Choose to faint not; don't let the little things wear you out.
Faint not, that's what this faith-walk is all about.
Choose to faint not; it is a choice you need to make,
because sometimes you can have your ice cream and
your cake too.

Looking Through the Eyes of Faith.

We hear the words, "Walk by faith, not by sight."
Looking through the eyes of faith is a faith fight.
When the tests come and the trials, too,
looking through the eyes of faith is not easy to do.
The bills are coming in the mail every day.
Looking through the eyes of faith will pave the way.
During the hard times, family and friends offer advice and much talk.
Looking through the eyes of faith: it is a faith walk.
We must focus on the word; it is our lifeline.
Looking through the eyes of faith will renew your mind.
Keep your eyes on Jesus; He looks from above.
Looking through the eyes of faith: see His amazing love.
Stay focused, resist the devil; he will flee.
Looking through the eyes of faith will bring you total victory.
Put on the full armor of God; it will quench those fiery darts.
Looking through the eyes of faith; it's time to do your part.
Looking through the eyes of faith opens your spiritual eyes.
Now you can see that having faith brings wisdom and makes you wise.
Whatever state of life you find yourself in, learn to be content.
Looking through the eyes of faith, trusting in Jesus, our Savior: heaven sent!
Looking through the eyes of faith: joy comes and washes away the pain.
Looking through the eyes of faith: see the glory of our Lord, He reigns!

Build Your House on the Rock.

Jesus tells the story of a man who built his house on the rock:
the winds blew.
The thunder and rain came, too.
His house stood strong; it did not fall.
It was his faith in Jesus that held up those walls.
He also tells the story of the man who built his house
on the sand.
The winds blew and the rain came; it swept his house right
off the land.
Now, let me break it down for you.
This is what Jesus wants you to do:
read the word; get the right information.
Build your house (life) on Jesus; that is your foundation.
You see the storms of life will come and try to sweep you away.
Trust Jesus as your foundation: he will help you stay.
Stay faithful, strong, obedient, and live right.
Go forth, walking by your faith, not by sight.

Life: Living in Faith Every Day.

Life: living in faith every day.
Life: it gives God the space to have his say.
Psalms 36:9: "For with thee is the fountain of life: in thy light shall we see light."
Life: we walk by faith and not by sight.
Proverbs 3:24: "Yea, though shall lie down, and thy sleep shall be sweet."
Life like that can't be beat.
Habakkuk 2:4: "but the just shall live by his faith." We live by faith every day.
Yes, faith in Jesus, there is no other way.
Life: living in faith, all doubts will cease.
Romans 8:6: "For to be carnally minded is death; but to be spiritually minded is life and peace."
Life: living in faith every day; putting God first.
John 6:35: "And Jesus said unto them, I am the bread of life; He that cometh to me shall never hunger; and he that believeth on me shall never thirst."
Life: living in faith every day, for our God is faithful and just.
Romans 8:31: "What shall we then say to these things? If God be for us, who can be against us?"

Stop and Pause.

The bills are behind, nothing but lack,
and that old devil is on your back
whispering his lies and having his say.
Stop and pause: why are you listening to him, anyway?
Stop and pause: how did you forget?
Jesus fed the poor and healed the sick.
Take a pause; he is the one who meets every need.
And when we plant, he waters the seeds.
Stop and pause: all is well, nothing lost.
Jesus died for us; he paid the cost.
Everything that we go through makes us strong.
Stop and pause: you can hold on.
Speak to that mountain, tell it to go.
Now stop and pause; walk into your overflow.
If you will stop and pause, do it God's way,
blessings will overtake you and you can have what you say!

Faith to Hold On.

What we need is faith to hold on.
Faith to hold on; sometimes things go from right to wrong.
Faith to hold on when it looks like it is the end.
Faith to hold on; God does his best work then.
Faith to hold on; now there's the power.
Faith to hold on; He is the man of the hour.
Faith to hold on; you feel like giving up.
Faith to hold on; you need God to replenish your cup.
Faith to hold on: confident, knowing that He is on your team.
Faith to hold on; it will bring Him on the scene.
Faith to hold on; the bills are all behind.
Faith to hold on; knowing it is in God's time.
Faith to hold on; we need it during those tests and trials.
Come on, enduring with a smile.
Faith to hold on; times can be tough.
Faith to hold on; you got Jesus, and that is enough.
Hebrews 10:23; "Let us hold fast the profession of our faith without wavering;" let faith work for you.
Faith to hold on; we put God first in everything that we do.

PRAY

Give Out, but Not Giving In.

Sometimes when those tests and trials come, they come quick,
and there is no quick fix.
You must pray and faithfully press,
knowing that God will bring you out of this mess.
Give out, but not giving in.
Refusing that bait that leads you back into sin.
If we will heed what the Word of God has to say.
It will lead and guide us along the right way.
Give out, but not giving in; oh what to do?
Bursting out strong; it's the Christ in you!
Sickness will lead to weakness and bring you down.
All those bills, making your head spin around and around.
Give out, but not giving in; choosing to walk by faith
and trust,
storing up treasures that will not wither, nor rust.
Give out, but not giving in.
When we walk by faith, we will win!

He Lives!
(a play)

Scene 1

Narrator: As our story begins, we see Jesus entering the
Garden of Gethsemane to pray.
He asked his disciples to watch as he lay.
Bending and falling on his face,
He prayed for God's mercy and grace.

(*Jesus lies prone in prayer to God; He looks up and says:*)

Jesus: "If possible, let this cup pass from me.
Nevertheless, what will be, will be."

Narrator: Jesus came to check on the disciples, they
were asleep.
They awoke when He spoke.

Jesus: "Watch and pray, the spirit is willing, but the
flesh is weak."

Narrator: After praying three times, Jesus told his disciples to
rest, as the hour was at hand.
Judas about to betray the Son of Man.
He approached Jesus, daring to take a risk,
and gave Him such a loving kiss.
Although Judas smiled wearing such a fake mask, his betrayal
wouldn't last, even though the soldiers held Jesus fast.

(*Soldiers grab Jesus. Peter follows closely by.*)
Narrator: The soldiers took Jesus to be tried.
Jesus wasn't worried about all the lies.

They put a crown of thorns upon his head.
He was beaten raw until he bled.
The soldiers bowed, went down on their knees:
they praised and mocked Him with sarcasm and much glee.
"Hail, King of the Jews," they would say.
They were determined that things go their way.

(*The soldiers continue to beat and mock Jesus.*)

Scene 2

Narrator: Meanwhile, Peter was denying Jesus Christ.
All his bragging and yet he could not pay the price.
A young lady looked at Peter and said:
"You are one of His disciples; you always followed wherever He led."

Peter: "I tell you no lie! I do not know that guy!"

Narrator: As Peter warmed himself by the fire, he was asked again:
"Aren't you one of His disciples, one of His trusted friends?"

Peter: "I tell you no lie! I never followed that guy!"

Narrator: A servant of the High Priest spoke and made his words very clear:
"Hey, aren't you that brave disciple in the garden who cut off my cousin's ear?"

Peter: "I tell you no LIE! I do not know that GUY!"

Narrator: He hears a bird crow.
Peter drops his head, for, he knows.

Three times he has denied knowing His savior and best friend! Could there be a greater sin?

(Peter quickly runs away, broken and hurt.)

Scene 3

Narrator: Jesus was stripped, spit on and beaten: so much pain!
But through it all, he was faithful: never doubtful, and never ashamed.
The multitude, the priests, and the elders wished Him crucified.
They were not expecting or ready for an awesome surprise!

(The soldiers carry a weak Jesus to the cross to be crucified. Mary, the mother of Jesus, Mary Magdalene, Luke, and John are crying as they stand and watch Him hang from the cross.)
(Dramatic music plays, then ends. Jesus speaks:)

Jesus: "Hallelujah, Hallelujah! Lord, forgive them for they know not what they do.
Here is my spirit; I give it to you! It is finished!"

(Jesus bows His head and dies.)

Narrator: Nicodemus and Joseph took Jesus' body, dressed him in clean linen cloth and buried him in Joseph's tomb. A stone was rolled in front to block and double lock the burial room.
Now some Pharisees came to Pilate and said, "Remember when Jesus said that in three days, he would rise? Let's seal the tomb for his disciples may steal his body and tell people these lies."

And so, Pilate said, "Have your way.
Put the guards there without delay."

(*The guards arrive at the tomb. They laugh, joke around, and happily play games as the three days go by.*)

Scene 4

Narrator: And then the third day came, the guards were feeling pretty good.
He had not risen like the disciples said He would.
Suddenly, behold, a great earthquake shook the ground!
Some dead came to life and walked around!
And an angel of the Lord ascended down.
(*Angel enters.*)
He rolled the stone away; Jesus was no longer bound!
Those guards, who were far from being saints,
fell to the ground in a death-like faint.
(*Guards faint.*)

Narrator: When the guards sat up from their faint and looked with fearful eyes,
they quickly jumped up and ran away to spread their sinful lies.

(*Jesus walks from the tomb and goes into the city.*)

(*Mary, mother of Jesus, and Mary Magdalene come to the tomb and are wondering
who rolled the stone away and stole His body.*)

Mary Magdalene: "Where is He? Someone has taken my Lord away!
We came to worship at his tomb today."

Mary, mother of Jesus: (*weeping and upset*) "Yes, where is He? Oh, my, where have they taken Thee?"

Angel: "Why do you seek the living among the dead? Don't you remember what He said? He has risen!"

Narrator: Mary Magdalene went to tell the disciples that He had risen; He was not dead.
His greatest sacrifice was the blood He had shed.
Mary Magdalene, Mary, mother of Jesus, the disciples, and the angel rejoiced
and gave much praise!

(*"He Lives" plays. The two women and the angel rejoice in a praise dance. Luke, John, and the other disciples fall to their knees and lift their hands in worship!*)

The End.

If You Don't Pray, You Won't Stay.

If you don't pray, you won't stay.
This will give the devil room to have his way.
When it comes to praying, the Bible has a lot to say!
We see in His words that Jesus prayed every day.
He knew that if you don't pray, you won't stay.
He even taught his disciples how to pray.
If you don't pray, you won't stay; your flesh becomes weak.
You need to bend your knees and hear God speak!
If you don't pray, you won't stay; prayer is what you need.
Prayer keeps out all that dirt and all those growing weeds.
If you don't pray, you won't stay; you have no power.
Your life without prayer becomes stale and sour.
If you don't pray, you won't stay; your faith is dead.
Listen! Prayer is what keeps it fed.
Pray! You have so much to gain.
Prayer gives you the power to say, "My Lord, let it rain!"

Jesus Prayed!
(a celebration of National Prayer Day)

The four Apostles quote a scripture about the importance of prayer.
Matthew: Matt. 26:41: "Watch and pray, that you enter not into temptation: the spirit indeed is willing, but the flesh is weak."
(Pray and the flesh will pass the test.)

Mark: Mark 1:35: "and in the morning, rising up a great while before day, he went out, departed into a solidary place, and there prayed."
(Even Jesus had to pray to make it through each day.)

Luke: Luke 6:12: "And it came to pass in those days, that he went out into a mountain to pray, and continued all night in prayer to God."
(Sometimes it takes all night to win the fight.)

John: John 14:14: "If ye ask anything in my name, I will do it."
(Ask, believe, and receive.)
We pray.
Romans 1:9: "For God is my witness, whom I serve with my spirit in the gospel of his son; that without ceasing I make mention of you always in my prayers."
(I pray for you, you pray for me, and that is the way that it should be.)
Romans: 8:26: "Likewise the spirit also helpeth our infirmities: for we know not what we should pray for as we ought: but the spirit itself maketh intercession for us with groanings which cannot be uttered."

(The Holy Spirit leads and guides, He is the comforter of our lives.)

Philippians 4:6: "Be careful for nothing; but in everything by prayer and supplications with thanksgiving let your requests be known unto God."
(Come before the throne, you have earned the right, for you are precious in God's sight.)
1st Thessalonians 5:17: "Pray without ceasing."
(Let us pray every day, lest we become weak, for prayer is the answer to all that we seek.)

James 5:16: "Confess your faults one to another and pray one for another, that ye may be healed. The effectual prayer of a righteous man availeth much."
(A church family that prays for each other, forever covers the heads of their sisters and brothers.)

All: 2 Chronicles 7:14: "If my people, which are called by my name, shall humble themselves, and pray, and seek my face, and turn from their wicked ways, then will I hear from heaven, and will forgive their sins, and will heal their land."

Pray, Press, and Praise!

The word says tests and trials come to make you strong; I now find this to be true.
If you will allow me, I would like to share this wisdom with you.
The struggles of life pummel you like tidal waves.
You need to pray, press, and praise!
1st Thessalonians 5:17 says, "Pray without ceasing." It is a must.
Prayer will release God's power and bring His trust.
Matthew 26:41: "Watch and pray that you enter not in temptation…" for the flesh is weak.
Pray, press, and praise: the Lord's face you must seek.
Proverbs 15:29: "but he heareth the prayers of the righteous," His ear is close to them.
Pray, press, and praise: we should place our faith in Him!
Romans 12:12: "Rejoicing in hope; patient in tribulation; continuing instant in prayer," it is the key.
It will work for you; it worked for me!
The tests and trials will come, yes, they will.
Remember this walk is not based on what you feel.
Psalm 145:3: "Great is the Lord, and greatly to be praised." We lift our hands and raise our voice.
Pray, press, and praise: it is up to you to make the right choice.
Pray, press, and praise: seasons come, and seasons go.
Pray, press, and praise: walk into your overflow!

Press and Pray!

We go through tests and trials every day.
Yes, that is why we have to press and pray.
Pray through the pain, suffering, and sometimes a broken heart.
We pray faithfully for God to step in and for that devil to depart!
1st Thessalonians 5:17 says, "Pray without ceasing."
These three powerful words help you to pray and press on, faith ever increasing.
Press and pray through every test.
God will come along and bring you rest.

You come to church and sit in your usual seat,
but the Holy Spirit presses you to jump to your dead feet!
"Press and pray." These words ring clearly within your head.
Suddenly, you remember a scripture that your Bible said:
"The race is not given to the swift, nor to the strong, but to the one who endures" and hangs on.
Press and pray, press and pray, you need to press and pray your way out.
Press and pray. Get ready for a victory shout!

You've Got to Pray!

Matthew 21:22: "If you believe, you will receive whatever you ask for in prayer."
You've got to pray; He will answer with tender loving care.
Psalm 27:8: "My heart says of you, seek his face! Your face, Lord, I will seek."
You've got to pray; your soul He will keep.
Mark 14:38: "Watch and pray so that you will not fall into temptation.
The spirit is willing, but the flesh is weak."
You've got to pray; that untamed flesh can lead to your defeat.
John 15:7: "If ye abide in me, and my words abide in you, ye shall ask what you will, and it shall be done unto you."
You've got to pray; God will bless everything you put your hands to do!
Psalm 37:4: "Delight thyself also in the Lord; and he shall give thee the desires of thine heart."
You've got to pray; do your part.
Colossians 4:2: "Continue in prayer, and watch in the same with thanksgiving."
You've got to pray! It is the power we need for daily living.

THE DEVIL IS A LIAR

Devil, I Am Not Coming Down.
(Living on the Higher Level)

Troubles, circumstances, trials, and tests: they are a must.
During these times, we need to hear the words God has for us.
Don't let the enemy distract you, bringing you doubt.
The word says that God will bring you out.
Tell the devil: you are not coming down.
You are living on a higher level: heaven bound.
Living on a higher level, God will fill our cup.
We won't come down; let the God in us rise up.
Face the facts but don't let the truth go.
Let me tell you something that you need to know.
Facts are subject to change, but the fact is,
The truth remains the same.
Remember, God puts no more on us than we can bear.
Trust Him; live on the higher level and stay there.
Lift you head up; don't let the enemy drag you down.
Live on the higher level, heaven bound.

Devil, I Am Not for Sale.

Step back, Devil; let me set the record straight.
I already told you: I won't take the bait.
There have been times when I stumbled, almost fell.
But I am still standing, Devil, I am not for sale.
You can't buy me, or put me on the auction block.
Jesus is my owner; He is my rock.
I know your tricks; you are full of lies and deceit.
Yea, you come like a thief, you sneak and creep.
You are always ready to pounce on the helpless and weak.
Devil, step off; God made me strong.
You can't buy me; *click*, I'm hanging up the phone!
I am not for sale! Can you hear?
I am not for sale! I'm saying it loud and clear.
Jesus shed His precious blood for me; He paid the price.
Devil, I am not for sale! I belong to Jesus Christ!

Don't Let Sin Sneak Back In.

You're saved, sanctified, and filled with the Holy Ghost.
Above all else, you love God the most.
The Lord is pleased; it makes Him glad,
but that old devil, boy, is he mad!
He had you once; he wants you again.
Don't let sin sneak back in.
Keep your guard up; watch what you say
because Satan is waiting to step in and have his way.
Don't you let sin sneak back in; kick it out.
You better not let the devil steal your shout.
When you let sin sneak back in, here comes the shame
and Satan is the only one who gets the fame.
Keep sin out, read God's Word and pray,
for He will help you stay sin-free every day.

Don't Take the Bait (of Satan).

Stop! Watch out! Listen, and beware,
for the bait of Satan is out there.
The bait will bring about unforgiveness, cause love to die.
This bait will make you steal, scheme, and lie.
This bait of Satan is poisonous, making you hateful and mean.
It will make you feel dirty and unclean.
Don't take the bait; it will grow roots of doubt.
Don't take the bait; spit it out!
When the devil brings his bait, run the other way.
Allow the Holy Spirit to lead you as you pray.
Even when Satan brings his bait, remember, it is not too late
to step on his head and seal his fate.
You don't have to be a brain in your school
To know that God, not Satan, is the one who rules.
Satan will bring offenses and his dirty bait to you.
Don't take the bait; it will make you sick.
God can bring the healing touch, quick, quick, quick!
Don't take the bait; pray your way through.
God has given you victory in all that you do.
Don't take the bait; Satan is so lame!
He doesn't know when he has lost his game.

Don't Buy the Lie.

"Girl, have some fun, live your life. You're young, you've got time."
Don't buy the lie; see the signs.
"God understands when I cheat and steal.
He knows that I have to do what I can to live."
Don't buy the lie; all the bad things we do are sins.
You can't live like that and expect to win.
"Man, ain't nothing wrong with getting a little high."
If you believe that, you just bought the lie.
"Come on, let's have a little chat.
Now, I know you are saved, but it don't take all that."
Don't buy the lie; God made a pact.
And to receive it, it will take this and that.
It is time to receive it, don't wait.
Don't buy the lie; don't take the bait.
Don't buy the lie; stop being on the run.
Don't buy the lie; living for God is a whole lot of fun!

Don't Go to Hell from the Pew.

Sitting there, acting like you are all that; no one can tell you what to do.
Don't you go to hell from the pew.
Your head is turning left and right.
You focus to keep everyone in your sight.
Lift your hands in a form of praise, always on cue.
Don't you go to hell from the pew.
The pastor is preaching; you are talking
about how you need to be walking out the door.
You show up late, like you are doing God a favor.
Don't you know that salt is no good when it loses its savor?
The word is coming forth, but you can't hear.
How can you receive what you don't hold dear?
Don't go to hell from the pew.
Many are called; seek to be the chosen few.

Show the Devil the Door.

The devil comes to steal everything from you that he can.
It is his desire to make you disobey all that God commands.
He is sneaky, lowdown, and always ready to pounce.
So, you better not give him one inch, not one ounce.
Show that devil the door.
That old devil likes to start all kinds of trouble.
Show him the door on the double.
He will try to fool you with all his lies,
But our God says, "We are to be watchful and wise."
Show the devil the door, it will set you free.
Learn to walk by faith, not by what you see.
Show the devil the door, put up a "Do not Enter" sign.
Now the light of God's glory can truly shine.
Show the devil the door, put him out!
Get those hands up and give a victory shout.

"Sin Ain't Your Friend."

James 4:7 says, "Submit yourself and resist the devil, and he will flee."
Let all ears be opened to hear, your eyes opened to see.
The devil comes to steal, kill, and destroy; it is his job.
Every promise God has made to you, he seeks to rob.
He wants to pull you back into sin.
Listen up: "Sin ain't your friend."
It will whisper in your ear just like a lover,
but when the lights come on, it will duck for cover.
Sin ain't your friend; it will leave you alone.
Sin will kill, steal, and destroy your home.
As Christ died for our sins,
there's no way it can be your friend.
Be wise, hear my wisdom, get the understanding: "Sin ain't your friend."
Turn away from it and don't do it again.
Don't buddy up with that nasty old sin.
He's a liar and a thief; he ain't your friend.
Warning! Be alert! "Sin ain't your friend."
Cut the blinds, walk free; it's the only way to win.

Sin is Like a Bag of Smelly Garbage.

Sin is like a bag of garbage: it smells bad.
You try to hide it, but the smell is so foul, it makes you mad.
You smile on the outside, cry on the inside.
This smell you cannot hide.
That smelly sin won't let you sleep;
don't you know that you can only reap what you sow?
When you sow to the flesh,
your smelly trash becomes a smelly mess.
Come on, take that smelly stuff and throw it away.
Jesus forgives sin; there is no price for you to pay.
Give it to Him; he is the only one who can clear the smell.
Jesus is the garbage man; he tells sin to go.
When He washes you, he cleans you whiter than snow.

Take Heed, Don't be Deceived.

Listen up: take heed, don't be deceived.
Walk in what you know and believe.
Deception is Satan's device to lead you astray.
So wise up and do things God's way.
Take heed; don't be deceived: the devil is always around,
plotting and scheming to bring you down.
Don't be deceived; watch out for his traps.
Take heed; sometimes he comes with just a little tap.
Listen up; be wise, it's up to you.
Just what you allow the devil to do.
Take heed; don't be deceived, and get this in your head:
flesh must die, and it must stay dead.
Take heed; don't be deceived, just chill.
We walk by faith, not by what we feel.
If you take heed, you won't be deceived, but ever aware
That God loves you and will always be there.

The Devil is a Liar.

You know the devil is a liar.
He wants to put you in the fire.
Don't be fooled by what he says;
By the spirit, you are led.
He has a lot of bark, but no bite.
He seeks to steal your holy light.
So be wise about whose voice you hear:
one works to give you courage, the other, fear.
The devil has no friends.
He wants to reel you in
to a life of hurt and pain,
and make you a prisoner of shame.
Listen to what I'm saying:
we all must be praying.
The devil is a liar.
He wants to put you in the fire.
Say God's words all the time.
Don't let the devil inside your mind.
Don't believe what he is saying.
We must all keep on praying!
The devil is a liar.
He wants to put you in the fire.
That devil: he's a liar.
Don't let him put you in the fire.

The Flesh is a Mess!

Trials, tribulations, situations; no matter what the test,
the bottom line is: the flesh is a mess.
Romans 8:8: "So then they that are in the flesh cannot
please God."
There is no need to try and reason with the flesh;
that will only lead to confusion and unrest.
We are to crucify the flesh daily, don't let it win.
Because, given a chance, it will lead us back to sin.
The flesh will tell you everything you want to hear.
The flesh will cause you to live in fear.
The flesh will beg, plead, and whine.
Because, you see, the flesh wants to rule your body and
your mind.
Jesus said: the spirit is willing, but the flesh is weak.
Don't give in to it, for it could be your defeat.
1 Peter 2:11 states it plain and bold:
"Dearly beloved, I beseech you as strangers and pilgrims,
abstain from fleshy lust,
which war against the soul."
The flesh will take you on a sin-filled ride.
And then, when the grits hit the fan, it will run and hide.
The flesh will have you waking up in the wrong bed.
The flesh will not allow you to use your head.
The flesh is a mess, don't be fooled.
Its main goal is to make sure you lose.
Galatians 5:16: "This I say then, walk in the spirit, and ye shall
not fulfill the lust of the flesh."
Because when you walk in Jesus, you walk with the best.

GET YOUR MIND IN LINE!

Don't be Derailed.

In this walk, times can be hard and may get a little rough.
You are sick and tired; you've had enough.
You look for someone to blame.
Because now you are feeling alone and ashamed.
You try to be strong, but you are weak.
It's about to make you freak!
There is no doubt; it's a fact:
your mind is under attack.
Don't be derailed, get back on track.
God has already broken the devil's back.
Don't be derailed, pray down those walls.
Jesus is on the main line; give Him a call.
Don't be derailed; put up a Holy Ghost fight.
Remember we walk by faith, not by sight.
Your faith will go on trial.
Don't be derailed; trust God and just smile.
Trusting God will help you grow.
And, yes, it will bring you overflow.
Don't be derailed; claim your prize.
Stay faithful and keep your eyes
on Jesus.

Get Wisdom; Get Understanding.

Proverbs 4:5: "Get wisdom, get understanding; forget it not."
Wisdom with understanding will aid you and help you,
when God's wisdom is taught, caught, and got.
Proverbs 4:6: "Forsake her not, and she shall preserve thee;
love her and she shall keep thee."
Wisdom with understanding is the door, lock, and key.
Proverbs 4:7: "Wisdom is the principal thing; therefore, get
wisdom; and with all thy getting;
get understanding."
Life without wisdom can be hard and demanding.
Proverbs 4:8: "Exalt her, and she shall promote thee: she shall
bring thee to honor,
when thou dost embrace her."
Embrace wisdom and understanding; it will wrap you up like
a warm, comfortable fur.
Proverbs 4:9: "She shall give to thine head an ornament of
grace: a crown of glory shall
she deliver to thee."
When we ask God for wisdom and understanding, it will be
given to you and given to me.
Proverbs 4:12: "When thou goest, thy steps shall not be hindered; and when thou runnest, thou
shall not stumble."
Get wisdom, get understanding, ask of the God who never
sleeps nor slumbers.
James 1:5: "If any of you lack wisdom, let him ask of the God,
that giveth to all men liberally and upbraideth not; and shall
be given him."
Get wisdom and understanding: it is like a cup pouring out,
spilling over the rim.

Colossians 3:16: "Let the word of Christ dwell in you richly in all wisdom." Let that wisdom
dwell richly in you.
Get wisdom and understanding; use it richly in everything that you do.
Proverbs 16:16: "How much better is it to get wisdom than gold! And to get understanding
rather to be chosen than silver!"
Get wisdom, get understanding; use it like a deep, flowing river.

Get Your Mind in Line.

So much is happening; all of your time just seems to fly away.
Satan is prowling around, seeking to steal the rest of the day.
He takes every chance to put crazy thoughts in your mind.
It is a battle to keep your mind in line.
His focus is to take your peace: it's all a game.
His goal is to drive you insane.
If you get your mind in line, and
search the word, you will find, there is help every time.
The best thing to do is, "Let your mind be in Christ."
He alone should rule because he paid the price.
Live in the new; shrug off the old.
To Him, let your mind be sold.
Focus, pray: do all you can to get your mind in line.
For we need the light of victory to break through and shine.
Here's a lesson for you to learn and do
when your mind plays tricks on you:
Trust in God; He will keep your mind in line
by filling you with His spirit and renewing your mind.
You see, God loves it when we think right.
Our minds have to be in line to win the fight.
Remember this: if you seek, you will find
that perfect peace to keep your mind in line.

Grow Up!

When the Word of God is planted, let us receive it and sow.
It will help us to mature and grow.
Let the word fill your hungry soul.
Get off that milk; you are too old.
The Word of God is what you should seek.
Put that bottle down; eat some meat.
It's time to grow up; repent from your sins.
Get full of the spirit and live as grown women and men.
We know that old devil wants you to stay a helpless child.
Grow up; he is a conniving liar, evil and most foul.
Grow up,; stand wise, stand strong.
In Jesus' arms is where you belong.
Grow up; time out for childish games.
We serve a God that loves us and knows our names.
We are apple of God's eye.
Grow up and know that He is not a man that should lie.
Grow up in Jesus; haven't you heard?
The power you need is hearing and doing the word.
When the seeds of the word are planted, you need to continue to sow.
Because when you sow, you will grow.
Grow up; don't let your life slip away.
Grow up; be willing and obedient to live for God, everyday!

Hearing Mess Will Mess You Up.

All kinds of thoughts going through your head:
keeping you from focusing on what the Word of God said.
Knowing that "weeping may endure for a night,"
but all these negative thoughts have blinded the light.
Yes, you know that God shall supply all your needs.
But what you see ain't nothing but weeds.
Hearing mess will mess you up,
making it hard for God to fill your cup.
The devil, whispering in your ear
trying everything to bring the fear.
Your family offering no help at all,
cutting you short when you give them a call.
Hearing mess will mess you up, bring you down.
You can't hear God, not even a sound.
Your so-called friends, knowing you are in lack,
talking and laughing behind your back.
And of course, the devil makes sure that you know what they said,
messing with your mind and your head.
Hearing mess will mess you up; close that can.
Hear God's words, seek to understand.
Hearing mess will mess you up: be careful what you hear.
Hear what God is saying, for His words are true and sincere.

How Can I Hear You?

Clutter, worries, sickness, all clouding my mind,
blocking my ears; no peace that I can find.
Trials, tests, and turmoil: I try to escape,
and yes, I've had about all I can take.
What to do in the midst of all this mess?
I'm feeling alone and doubtful, I must confess.
How can I hear what you are saying?
Please, don't even talk about fasting and praying.
That old devil tries to use every trick to bring me down.
Here I stand, not making a sound.
How can I hear you with so much going on?
I ask myself, "Do I even belong?"
How can I hear or even see?
Then, I realize that the one in the way is me.
How can I hear you? "Lord unstop my ears,
quench the fiery darts, bind my fears."
How can I hear you? I need to know.
I am ready for blessings to flow.
How can I hear? I found the key.
Recognize that in Christ, you are free.
Love Him; trust Him. Every day of the year.
I ask you now, "Can you hear?"

I've Got to Get This Right.

Tossing, turning, worrying, no sleep at night.
One thing I do know, I've got to get this right.
I've got to get this right, time out for games;
living like this is driving me insane.
I have no peace, no joy, there is no rest.
I am being defeated by every test.
The battle is not mine, yet I still fight.
What can I say? I've got to get this right.
Time out for playing the field;
I've got to get this right, time to be real.
I've got to get this right; time is winding up.
I've got to get this right; choose the right way.
I've got to get this right; I'll do it today.
My eyes are open, now I can see.
Whom the son sets free is also for me.
I reach out for God's hand and know I can get this right.
And then help others to see the light.

Isaiah 1:19.

Isaiah 1:19: "if ye be willing and obedient, ye shall
eat the good
of the land."
Willing and obedient: start by receiving and obeying
this command.
Learn how to be willing and obedient and you will receive.
Now this kind of faith comes when you are willing to believe.
God wants to pour out continual overflows,
but you must allow Him to not just open but close
some doors.
Willing and obedient; the mind of Christ is what is you need.
It takes His mindset to uproot those weeds.
Willingness comes from deep within your heart,
but being willing and obedient together plays a big part.
A willing heart, yes, God is pleased!
Now, you are ready to receive.
Be willing to do and willing to obey.
Let your willing and obedient actions pave the way.
Be willing and obedient: they make a powerful team.
Try it and watch God show up on the scene.
Be willing and obedient to confess your sins, and salvation
you will receive.
When you are willing and obedient, you will not allow the
devil to deceive.
Be willing and obedient, you know you should.
Be willing and obedient, it is your time to eat the good!

It's About the Thought Life.

Seek to be good ground, keep those thoughts right.
You see, bad thoughts will steal your faith fight.
Good thoughts can liberate you.
Wrong thoughts can bring bondage and stick like glue.
Wrong thinking starts with a wrong seed.
Seeds that grow and grow, sprouting those weeds.
Good thoughts will feed your soul.
Good thoughts will lead you down a perfect road.
Don't allow the enemy to block your mind.
Trust God to guide your thoughts, He is the powerline.
Every vain thought, cast it down.
For the mind God gave you, it is sound.
It's about your thought life, what you think can bless or have you in a mess.
It's about your thought life: think right!
Good thoughts come when we walk by faith and not by sight.
It's about your thought life; take the time.
Read God's Word, pray, and get your thought life; take your time.
It's about your thought life, seek good thoughts and you will find
that God's peace and joy will rule your mind.

Mind Under Construction.

They say the mind is a terrible thing to waste,
yet you dare to get up in my face,
talking about "everything is all right."
Well, if that is the truth, where is your light?
Your mind is on this, then on that, and then this again.
You need to get your mind right if you want to win.
Your mind needs to be under construction; do it now.
Read God's Word; it will show you how.
Study the word; meditate on it day and night.
Do whatever it takes to get your mind right.
Don't forget to fast and pray,
asking God to renew your mind every day.
A mind is a terrible thing to waste.
Get God on your mind and see that He is good.

Perhaps You Have Heard These Proverbs?

Proverbs 1:7 says, "The fear of the Lord is the beginning of knowledge,
but fools despise wisdom and instruction."
In other words: not fearing God is a path to death and destruction.
Proverbs 3:13 says, "Happy is the man that findeth wisdom and the man
that getteth understanding."
He will be the one to follow what God is commanding.
God said that never again would He destroy the world by flood, and in
Proverbs 6:17: "that he hated a proud look, a lying tongue, and
hands that shed innocent blood."
Proverbs gives advice and ways to live right.
Proverbs 12:22 says, "Lying lips are an abomination to the Lord: but they
that deal truly are in his delight."
Proverbs 10:12: "Hatred stirreth up strife...."
Proverbs 14:27 says, "The fear of the Lord is foundation of life...."
Our mouth should not curse and then sing a spiritual song.
For Proverbs 18:21 says, "Death and life are in the power of the tongue."
Don't treat your sins lightly; listen to God's words.
He is talking to us through the Proverbs!
I will leave you with these two:
Remember, God loves and wants to save you.
Proverbs 28:13: "He that covereth his sin shall not prosper: but whoso
confesseth and forsaketh them shall have mercy."

Proverbs 18:10: "The name of the Lord is a strong tower: the righteous
Runneth into it and is safe."

Swat It Off (Let It Go).

Swat it off; move on with God, let it go.
We have to walk in peace, don't you know?
Swat them off, the lies that have been told.
Forget it; move on, you are on a new road.
Swat it off, it doesn't matter what people say.
Let God's spirit lead the way.
Don't give Satan any room in your heart.
Swat it off, let evil depart!
Swat them off, the worries and doubts.
Keep your peace; let the praise out!
Swat it off; move on with God, let it go.
We have to walk in peace, don't you know?

What Are You Saying?

"I don't know what I am going to do!"
"My mind is messed up and I am, too."
"Girl, I need a man to help me."
"You know you got to give it up, ain't nothing free."

What is coming out of your mouth: what are you saying?
Be quiet, get on your knees, and start praying.
What are you saying? Your mind is messed up.
Ask God to renew your mind, fill your cup.

Watch what you say: the wrong words can hurt you.
They will bring doubt, depression, and sickness, too.
What are you saying? Are you speaking what you believe?
Because what you say is what you will receive.

God hears what you say, and the devil does, too.
His goal is revive the old and kill the new.
What are you saying? No more words of doubt.
God's words are in you; let them come out!

Wise Up.

Every Christian needs to wise up.
Ask God for His wisdom, fill your cup.
You see, God wants you to be wise,
because when you wise up, you won't be so quick to believe the devil's lies.
Wise up; kill the flesh, it must die.
Wise up and break that soul tie.
Wise up; seek to please God in every way.
When you wise up, His wisdom will lead you every day.
Proverbs 4:7 says, "Wisdom is the principal thing; therefore get wisdom." It is the key.
It will break off the yokes and keep you free.
Wise up; let God renew your mind.
God's wisdom is worth the find.
Wise up: hear God's wisdom and heed to His call.
Get His understanding; you don't know at all.
Wise up; here's the deal:
wisdom is not walking by what you feel.
Wise up; trust God in all that you do.
Use His wisdom and stop letting the devil make a fool of you.
Do you seek to overcome divisions and strife?
Wise up; for wisdom is a tree of peace and life.
Hold on to wisdom, embrace it, receive it: it is more precious than gold.
Wise up; take a trip down the wisdom road.
Wise up; you need to know.
You have just walked into your overflow.

CHRISTMAS POETRY

A Christmas Miracle.
(*a play*)

List of Characters:
Narrator:
Gabriel:
Mary:
Joseph:
Angels:
Shepherds:
3 Wise men:
King Herod:
Jesus:
Satan (devil):

Scene 1

Narrator: Our story begins with Mary sitting quietly and humming to herself. Suddenly, an angel appears and speaks to her:

Gabriel: "Hail, sweet Mary, you have found favor with God and are blessed.
Of all women, you have passed the test."

(*Mary looks up, confused and afraid.*)

Gabriel: "Fear not, for God wants you to bring forth his son.
And put all this sin on the run."

Mary: (*still confused*) "No, no, this can't be.
I have known no man as you can see."

Gabriel: "The Holy Ghost will come upon you.
There is nothing you need to do.
He will be called Jesus, the son of God.

And rule this world with an iron rod."

Mary: (*smiling now*) "I am the handmaid of the Lord, I have heard.
Let it be done, according to your word."

(*Gabriel leaves.*)

Mary: (*speaking in awe*) "My soul is filled with praise.
For my spirit, God has raised.
I shall be called blessed, for holy is His name.
From this day forth, I know I will never be the same."

Scene 2
(*Mary goes to greet Joseph. He is standing alone.*)

Narrator: Joseph finds out that his fiancé is with child, but he is not the one.
He decides to break up with her because of what he thought she had done.

(*He is upset and tells her that the wedding is off. Mary is hurt but she walks away quietly.
That night when Joseph is asleep, an angel comes to visit him.*)

Angel: (*standing over sleeping Joseph and talking to him*)
"Do what is right, lest any other man should boast.
The child she has conceived is of the Holy Ghost.
Marry her; you are the one who wins.
This holy child is the savior who will save His people from their sins."

Narrator: Joseph obeyed and made her his wife,
and forever changed the course of their life.

(*When Joseph awakes, he hurries to Mary's house to tell her that he is
going to marry her. They hug each other happily.*)

Scene 3

Narrator: Joseph made Mary his wife the very next day,
for he knew the Lord would have it no other way.
Then, it came time for all to be taxed, and so Joseph had to go back
to Bethlehem.
But by the time he had completed his work,
Mary had labor pains and began to hurt.
It was time for the baby to enter the world.
They tried to find room at the inns,
but all were full, no room to lend.
The innkeeper offered them a stable, and the child was born.
It was an amazing sight to see on that Christmas morn.

(*Mary wraps baby Jesus in swaddling clothing and places Him in the manger.
She sits while Joseph stands beside her with his hand on her shoulder.*)

(*The scene changes from the stable to a field where some shepherds are tending
their flocks. A light shines, an angel appears, the shepherds are afraid.*)

Angel: "Fear not, behold, I bring you tidings of great joy.
The savior is born, a holy boy.
You will find him wrapped in swaddling clothing and lying in a manger.
He has come to this world to save all souls from sinful danger."

(*More angels appear.*)

Angels: "Glory to God in the highest, peace and goodwill toward all men.
For tonight our savior is born, He will save us from their sins."

(*Angels leave.*)

Shepherd: (*excited*) "Let us go and see this thing that has come to pass.
For now, we can see our savior at last."

(*The shepherds find the baby and bow down and worship the holy child.
As they leave, they look back in awe at this wonderful sight.*)

Scene 4

Narrator: Some wise men heard of the newborn child.
They were excited, for they had traveled many miles.

Wise men: "Where is the king of the Jews? We have seen His star.
We want to worship Him; we have come from afar."

Narrator: King Herod heard them and was afraid that he would lose his rule,
and be left looking the fool.
He sent them to Bethlehem to worship the king,
but his thoughts were evil and mean. He told them:

King Herod: "Go, see this Christ child, and bring me word,
for I also want to know if it is true what I have heard.
Perhaps I will worship, too,
and bring Him gifts, the same as you."

Narrator: The wise men followed the star; it led them to holy child.
They were full of joy and drew near, all smiles.

(*They wise men bow as they each present their gift to the child.*)

1st Wiseman: "I present to your child a gift of gold."
2nd Wiseman: "I present my gift of frankincense."
3rd Wiseman: "I present to Him my gift of myrrh. We rejoice happily on His birth."

(*A worship song may be played during this scene. After the song ends, the
wise men stand and leave, bowing into the holy child.*)

Narrator: God had warned the wise men in a dream
of the evilness of Herod, the king.
The wise men decided to go another way.
They had nothing more to say.

Narrator: An angel came to Joseph and said:

Angel: (*enters*) "Flee into Egypt because Herod wants the child dead."

(*Angel leaves. Joseph and Mary travel to Egypt to avoid King Herod.*)

Scene 5

Narrator: "Eventually, they returned to Nazareth, their home,
where their holy child grew and became strong.
He was filled with God's spirit, wisdom, and grace.
God was preparing Him daily for the victorious race.

One day, Jesus, being full of the Holy Ghost, was led into the wilderness
for His first test.
He was there for forty days; he had no food or rest.

(*Jesus enters and sits down. The devil enters with a briefcase. He struts over
to Jesus. Jesus stands and moves His chair back.*)

Satan: "Listen, Jesus, I know you are tired and so I am ready to make you a deal.
Believe me when I say I didn't come to destroy and kill.
People love to put everything on the devil.
All I want to do is take you to a whole new level!
If thou be the son of God, command this stone to be made into bread,
for I heard that by the spirit you are led."

(*The devil holds a stone in his outstretched hand.*)

Jesus: "It is written: man shall not live by bread alone.
Now why don't you pack up your little briefcase and scurry back home?"

(*The devil drops the stone to the floor.*)

Satan: (*waves his hand all around the room*) "You can have command over
the whole world: I will give it to you.
Bow down and worship me is all you have to do."

Jesus: "Get thee behind me.
Your evil is what I see.

It is written: *thou shalt worship the Lord and him only shalt thou serve.*
And so, I worship and give Him all that he deserves."

Satan: (*takes Jesus up on a high place*) "If thou be the son of God, cast thyself down.
It was written, God gives his angels charge over thee and you won't hit the ground."

Jesus: "It is written, the Lord God, thou shalt not tempt.
You have no power, Satan; you are a wimp."

Satan: (*angry and defeated*) "I will be back, wait and see. No one makes a fool of me!"

Jesus: "Too late! Remember how foolish you looked falling from the sky?
Satan, you are the weakest link. Goodbye!"

(*Satan leaves and angels come surround Jesus. He speaks.*)

Jesus: "The spirit of the Lord is upon me.
God has anointed me to set the captives free.
I have come to open the eyes of the blind, and their ears, too.
I have come to take away all sins from you.
Today, harden not your hearts, hear my call.
Come one, come two, come all!"

(*Jesus opens his arms wide to welcome all who will come. As he leaves, the angels
follow bowing and praising him. A beautiful praise song played as Jesus and the angels
exit the scene.*)

A Christmas Miracle.

Listen, open up your ears:
do you hear what I hear?
A silent night, a joy to the world, and hark, the herald sings.
On this Christmas Day was born a savior and our king.
Shepherds from the fields came from afar.
They came to worship, following a bright star.
Wise men came bearing gifts; they wanted to see this wondrous sight.
King Herod was jealous and ready to fight.
He knew that the savior was here
and peace had come to those who had walked in fear.
A Christmas miracle, God has given us.
A savior full of love, in Him we put our trust.
A Christmas miracle; He took our sinful shame
and washed us clean: we will never be the same.
A Christmas miracle found throughout the year.
He comforts the hurt, heals the sick, and wipes away every tear.
A Christmas miracle; He went to the cross.
He redeemed and saved us that were lost.
A Christmas miracle; He came with mercy and love;
He was sent to us from God above.
He humbled Himself and paid the price.
He gave us his best gift: eternal life.
Hallelujah for our Christmas miracle, Jesus Christ!

A Christmas Welcome.

Welcome! It's Jesus' birthday.
I would like to say:
Happy Birthday, Jesus, we love you.
And we know you love us, too.
Welcome! It's your party, come on in.
Thank you for freeing us from sin.
Welcome! Have your way.
We welcome you on your birthday!

We Bow Down.

We have to come to worship and bow down.
To a king who will turn your life around.
We bow down to Him who reigns.
He is the Savior; Jesus is His name.
We bow down; only He can forgive sins.
We bow down; we worship; we win!

Picture This.

It was the day before Christmas, extremely cold.
Stores were packed out; cars and trucks cluttered the road.

Shoppers were searching to find that last minute gift,
catch a sale.
Some were willing to fight and go to jail!

Christmas should not make people lose their minds,
pushing and shoving to be first in line.

There was a song about "Santa Claus is Coming to Town."
Well, guess what? Jesus has always been around.

Talking about you better not cry, you better not pout.
You really don't have to when you realize what Christmas is
really about.

Jesus, our savior, was born on Christmas Day, that
we may live
stress-free at our Father's will.

So, as you are trying to fit all those gifts under the tree,
remember this: Jesus was born to set us free.

And so, on this precious Christmas Day, as you open each gift
and smile,
Tell Jesus, "Thank You," and say it good and loud.

Signs, Wonders, and Miracles, Oh My!

A shining star leads the way
to the birth of Jesus on Christmas Day.
Signs, wonders, and miracles, oh my!
His glorious birth lit up the sky.
Our wonderful savior, He was born to save the world from sin.
He never doubted that He would win.
Signs, wonders, miracles, oh my!.
He defeated Satan and made him cry.
Jesus fed the hungry and turned water into wine.
He healed the sick and gave sight to the blind.
Signs, wonders, and miracles, oh my!
He came that we might live and not die.
He offers salvation to the sin-sick, the lost.
He gave his life to hang on the cross.
Jesus did it all for you and me.
He wants us to know that "salvation is free."
Signs, wonder, and miracles, oh my!
We have no more reasons to wonder why.
Jesus was born on Christmas Day.
You see, He came to show us the way.
Jesus came to answer every call.
And when He died for us,
He gave the greatest sign, wonder, and miracle of all. Oh my!

The Perfect Gift.

Christmas Day, one, two,
many gifts for you and you.
Christmas Day, three, four.
Gifts all open, looking for more.
Christmas Day, five, six, and seven.
The Perfect Gift has come from heaven.
Christmas Day, eight, nine.
A more perfect gift you will not find.
Christmas Day, count to ten.
The savior has come to deliver us from sin.

Christmas Time.

It's Christmas time.
It makes me rhyme.
I think of Jesus born on this day.
Now I must have my say.
He came to heal, deliver, and set us free.
He came to be a savior for you and me.
He took away our shame.
There is power in His name.
Reach out, grab His hand.
His name is Jesus: the son of man.
It's Christmas time, it's Christmas time.
Praise to Him who makes me rhyme!

Christmas: The Savior is Born.

1st Child: "The savior is born,
born on Christmas Day.
He was wrapped in swaddling clothes
and in a manger, he lay."

2nd Child: "An angel told some shepherds outside of town
where the messiah could be found.
The shepherds worshipped Him and bowed down."

3rd Child: "Some wise men came with gifts, ready to worship the king.
The angels from heaven begin to sing."

All: "Our savior is born on this Christmas morn."

1st Child: "A star is shining, oh so bright.
It shines a pathway with its light,
The shepherds and wise men are led through the night.
It is the most glorious sight."

2nd Child: "A holy child, asleep on the hay.
He was born on Christmas Day.
His name is Jesus, they say.
He is the one who will pave the way."

3rd Child: "A star is shining on His face.
It leads all to his holy place.
A star is shining all around.
Bow and worship, you are on holy ground."

EASTER

Christ Got Up!

Christ got up; they couldn't keep Him down.
He rose; three days, no sound.
Christ got up and walked from His tomb, so bold.
Let His story now unfold and be told.

He went to the cross, suffered, asked God to forgive,
not to punish His enemies, but to let them live.
They pierced Him in His side,
buried him: a savior had died.

But in three days, He arose!
The disciples entered His tomb and found nothing but His burial clothes.
No one knew what to think,
but in one blink,
He stood before them, alive and well.
He was free from his burial cell.

Christ got up, not from the dust,
but he did get up for the sinners: us!
He got up! He got up! He is alive!
No kidding, no jive!

Christ got up; He lives today!
He is alive! What more can I say?

He Lives!

Hey, I have something to say!
Jesus is alive! He is here today.
Jesus Lives! Jesus Lives! He lives in me!

An Easter Welcome.

It's Easter Sunday and I would like to say:
welcome, welcome on this blessed day.
He went quietly and hung from the cross; what a price to pay.
We lift up our hands in praise and say, "Lord, have your mighty way!
It's Easter Sunday, and again I say:
welcome, welcome, enter in on this blessed day!

Jesus is Alive!

One, two, three.
Jesus died for you and for me!
Four, five, six.
To the cross, He went, for souls that He was out to fix.
Seven, eight, nine.
For every sin, He paid the fine!
Hands up for number ten.
I am saved! You are saved! I win, you win!

Good News.

Hey, have you heard the good news?
No more reason to sing the blues.
Jesus, He is alive!
Come on sister and brother, slap me five!

Yea, I know, He went to the grave.
Did you know: He rose in three days?
Listen up; He came to set us free!
Hallelujah, we are free to live in His victory!

Hey, have you heard the good news?
Don't be confused!
Jesus is alive!
Raise your hand, slap me a victorious high five!

He Lives!

You say, "He lives; He is not dead."
They say, "Come on, stop messing with my head."
You say, "He lives, inside our hearts and souls!"
They say, "I guess that is what you have been told."
You say, "He lives; He died and rose to set us free."
They say, "Maybe for you, but not for me."
You say, "In Christ I live, in Christ I die!"
They say, "You are telling a big old lie."
You say, "He lives, it is so clear."
They say, "Where? I can't see or hear him, is he near? Should I fear?"
You say, "He lives, hear me! Accept Him today!"
They say, "No, I'll live and do things my way."
You say, "He lives, He reigns, He rules!"
They say, "Being saved just ain't cool."
You say one last time, "He lives!" You say it loud!
"Listen to your heart and not this unbelieving crowd."
You say, "He lives, He lives! He rose on Easter Day!
It is the truth, there is nothing more to say."
He lives!

He was Born; He Died; and He has Risen!

Mary, the virgin that God chose: God will have His way!
She gave holy birth to Jesus on Christmas Day.
Jesus was born in an innkeeper's stable, and the shepherds traveled far.
They were led by God's bright, shiny star.
Jesus was born, full of grace, mercy, forgiveness, and love.
He came to save us; it was God's will being filled from above.
Jesus was born to carry out God's will.
It was to ensure that His every word be fulfilled.
Jesus was born to save me and to save you.
Accepting Him as your savior is all that we need to do.
Jesus knew that one day He must die.
For all who have read or heard His story, you know why.
Jesus gave His life; He went to the cross.
He died to bring salvation to all souls that were lost.
Jesus took the stripes upon His back.
It was to help us stay whole and healthy and free from the devil's attacks.
When Jesus died,
many lost sheep cried.
They took Him down and buried Him in Joseph's tomb.
It was just like the inn; there was no other room.
One day, two days, and then three.
Jesus arose from the grave; we were now set free!
Mary, Mary Magdalene, and Peter found no one inside.
They were worried that someone had took him for a ride.
An angel appeared to Mary and said, "Don't fear!
The one that you are looking for is not here.
He has risen; He is alive!
I tell you the truth, I speak no jive."

When Mary Magdalene happily saw Jesus, she joyfully went to hug Him, and Jesus said:
"Touch me not, for I have not ascended up.
I will send the comforter to fill your loving cup."
Jesus arose and sealed our believing fate.
He arose! Accept His gift; don't wait too late!
Jesus arose! He opened His arms and called us in.
He forgave and cleaned us up from all sins.
He arose Easter morning, ready to reach out and save the lost.
He had gladly paid the cost!
Jesus arose! Jesus arose! Give Him all your praise!
Every morning, every day, and every night, your hands you should raise!

In Three Days.

He was crucified; it was God's will
that Jesus died up on a hill.
The evil ones laughed at what they had done.
For you see, they thought that they had won.

The devil and his demons, they felt so crappy,
but now the party was on, and these guys were oh so happy.
"No more casting them out, giving sight to the blind, and
growing out legs."
This miracle worker is history, he is dead.

The tomb is sealed shut, two guards at the door.
They won't steal his body and cause an uproar.
One day, two days, three days came.
The guards became bored of this waiting game.

Suddenly, the ground shook with a big earthquake.
It was the third day, and Jesus was awake!

An angel appeared,; his clothes brilliant white.
His face was like lightning, shining bright.
The guards stood still, filled with fright.
And then fell in a dead faint at this glorious sight.

MISCELLANEOUS POETRY

Salute the "Real" Dads.

This salute is for the "real" dads, you know the ones, who take a stand
to be the best dads that they can.
To the "real" dads, not the ones who say, "I made a mistake."
Those kinds of dads never give; they just take and take and take!
A salute to dads who make their house a home,
a place of love where kids feel like they belong.
A salute to "real" dads who lead their children to walk upright.
They teach them to honor God who will give them strength for the fight.
"Real" dads love, encourage, praise their kids and are always there.
Sometimes they are the ones who must show them that tender-loving care.
We salute the single dads, striving to do their best,
for we know between their children and that job, there is no rest.
"Real" dads count it no loss.
They know and accept that sacrifice is worth the cost.
When "real" dads get into their place,
Real joy lights up their child's face!
Those "real" dads are something to see.
A "real" dad, all dads should seek to be.
Will the "real" dads proudly stand?
We salute you as "real" dads and as the real men!

A Woman of Few Words.

She is a woman of few words.
She needs no big audience to be heard.
The words that she speaks,
bring strength to the weak.
Her words of knowledge of Bible expressions
she uses to rebuke all forms of depression.

She is a woman of few words, this is true.
Her few words of God's power are just for you.
Words of wisdom, revelation, and light,
words that will lead you to live right.
Her words spoken, come from her heart and soul.
A few words of encouragement will make you
mighty and bold.

Yes, she is a woman of few words.
She needs no big audience to be heard.
She speaks only what she knows,
but those few words are as precious as gold.
For her faith is strong in her voice,
and the words she says, lead you to rejoice.

A woman of few words, she is not easy to find.
She is usually the one at the back of the line.
A woman of few words, it is the key.
A powerful woman with a powerful few words, I would
like to be!

Dead Man Walking.

Hey, you, yea you, with your head hanging down.
Your lips are moving, but I hear no sound.
I see your eyes, there is no light.
It's like looking at a blind man who has no sight.
And he answered, "What is it to you?
Leave me alone, there is nothing you can do!"
He dropped his head again and waited for me to leave.
He had nothing to live for and nothing to believe.
DEAD MAN WALKING!
Tears filled my eyes; I couldn't walk away.
The God in me had to have His say!
I reached out and touched his hand.
He pulled away, desperate to be the man.
I said three simple words: "God loves you!"
"When He died on the cross, he died for me and for you, too!"
His head popped up, he wanted to run,
but he knew that when it was all said and done
he would still be a DEAD MAN WALKING!
He opened his mouth and said these words: "My heart is
pained within me: and the terrors of death are fallen upon me."
It was Psalm 55:4; my heart ached in sympathy.
His eyes glittered with unshed tears,
as he confessed that he had been running from God for years.
DEAD MAN WALKING!
They are out there all around us.
Dead men walking, returning to dust.

Fathers.

Fathers, what can I say?
You see, they are also needed in every way.
Fathers: you see them walking around, everywhere,
but some find it hard to show their child tender-loving care.
Fathers take their sons to all the games.
They make sure for their little girls they do the same.
Fathers: they are proud to be the man,
even when they are struggling to do all they can.
Some fathers cook, wash clothes, and even clean.
They don't care about the "bling."
Fathers: they work hard to take care of home,
but some fathers leave the mothers to take care of their kids all alone.
Those kind of fathers can be something else,
acting like those babies got here themselves.
Thank God for good fathers who don't sit and sat,
lying around the house, eating, and getting fat.
Devoted fathers, taking their child by the hand,
and helping them to grow strong, able to strongly stand.
Young fathers: sometimes they stay, sometimes they run.
You see, they think that being a father will spoil their fun.
Old fathers: now, they can teach you fathers a thing or two,
about what all fathers are required to do.
It's Father's Day, let's make a scene.
Okay mothers, let me hear you thankfully scream:
"Happy Father's Day!"

Guard Your Heart.

Troubles will come and trials, too.
They won't last, they never do.
Things from your past: let them go.
We must guard our heart, don't you know?

People will talk, they always do.
It's not you they don't like; it's the God in you!
These are the times we need to be bold.
We must guard our hearts and our souls!

Guard your heart from jealousy and strife.
Guard your heart from the cares of life.
Guard your heart; God called you to be the light!
Guard your heart; obey Him, and live right.

Guard your heart; ask God to fill your cup.
Don't you know that the devil is always waiting for you to mess up?
He loves to whisper his lies in your ear.
He loves to cause your heart to tremble in fear.

Guard your heart; fill it with God's words of love and peace.
Guard your heart; crucify your flesh, and tame that carnal beast.
Guard your heart; lift His name up high!
Guard your heart and you will see our Savior burst through the sky!

"I Don't!" Until We Say, "I Do!"

"Man, I don't! until we say, "I do!"
Where is your mind and what is the matter with you?
I refuse to let you stay the night!
My eyes are open, I see the light.
So, what if he says, "I love you, why wait?"
No, no, don't take the bait.
You say to him, "Marry me; let's make this house a home,
or step out and be gone!"
"I don't until we say, I do."
Man, what is the matter with you?
You won't be crashing at my pad,
and have me waking up feeling lost and sad.
No more broken promises and paying a few bills.
I belong to God now and obey His will!
Yeah, you laughed, you thought it was all a joke.
Well, who is laughing now? Wow! Look at that Holy
Ghost smoke!
"I don't" until I hear and say, "I do."
Again, I say, man, what is the matter with you?
After the wedding vows and we say, "I do."
I will be willing to show you,
How blessed you are to be married to a queen.
"I do!" to my one and only, man of God, my hero,
and my king!

Moms.

Mother, ma, mum, maw, mummy: no matter which one they say.
Moms hear this coming from their child every day.
According to Genesis 3:20: God called Eve, the life-giving one and she was proud,
to be a wife and bring into the world her first born child.
Moms show patience and strength; they are the backbone.
You see a wise mom never tears down her home, even when she is left to raise her child alone.
Our kids tend sometimes to act blind, like they can't see.
How blessed they are to have moms like you and me!
Yes, moms do struggle, doing all they can,
Playing the role of the woman and, sometimes, the role of the man.
Moms, they brought all these fathers into the world,
and that is why a father can relate to that written precious song, "Thank Heaven for little girls."
Exodus 20:12 says, "Honour thy father and thy mother and thy days may be long upon the land."
It is not to be taken lightly; it is one of God's commands.
Moms must seek God and pray,
asking Him to always lead the way!
Moms, as you read God's words, keep this in mind:
moms are to be warm, caring, protective, loving and above all, kind.
On Mother's Day, Moms, go out, enjoy, or get you a much-needed rest.
Proverbs 31:28 says, "Her children arise up and call her blessed."
Happy Mother's Day, Moms!

Mothers.

Mothers: you see them everywhere.
They nurture their child or children with tender loving care.
Mothers: they are the ones going down that grocery aisle.
One hand holding a list, the other hand, a child.
Hey, look, there is a mother giving a hug.
Oh, she is smiling brightly, what love!
Mothers: cooking, cleaning, and washing those dirty clothes.
Yes, mothers do have many roles.
Some mothers work, some mothers stay at home.
Some mothers have to raise their kids alone.
Mothers: they do all that they can,
even without the help of the father, the man.
There are the church mothers, being an example; it is no surprise.
You see God made them patient and wise.
Tough mothers, taking the time,
To discipline and spank that child's behind.
Young mothers, find it not so easy to raise a child,
but soon they realize, it was all worthwhile.
Mothers, where would the fathers be?
If they didn't have mothers like you and me.
Mothers work, they comfort, and sometimes with little rest.
Nevertheless, Proverbs 31:28 says, "Her children arise up and call her blessed."
Mothers, be the mothers God has called you to be, it is His command.
On each Mother's Day, stand up and give yourself a hand.

What My Daughter Said.

My daughter said, "Mom, I think it is so whack,
how those bills collectors keep you under attack!"
I answered her and said, "Baby, I made those bills
and owe them,
but no need to worry, I have my peace in God, and I place all
faith in Him!"
She quickly replied, "I know your faith is strong,
and praying helps you to hold on!"
She said sadly, "I just get tired of not enough and so
much lack."
Hugging her close, I said, "Baby girl, God will never leave us,
and he has our back!"
My daughter smiled saying, "I heard that,
but I still think that those bill collectors are so whack!"
Laughing, I said, "Our God meets our needs and gives us
more than enough.
He is always around when times gets rough!"
"I trust Him, my daughter, you can too,
because what God does for me, He will do for you!"

WHAT IF?
(*a play*)

NARRATOR: Back in the Old Testament, God used great men and women of faith to fulfill His promises. These men and women of faith obeyed God without hesitation. But what if… What if when God asked Adam and Eve had they eaten from the Tree of Knowledge of Good and Evil, they had said—

ADAM: "Yes Lord, I did eat. You see this woman you gave me came with this delicious looking apple and she was looking so good holding it out to me. I completely lost my mind. I didn't ask her where she got the apple from, and I didn't care. But, God, she knew what she was eating. She seduced me and she should be severely punished. A woman has got to know her place and stay in it."

EVE: "Wait a minute! I know you are not trying to put all the blame on me. I didn't twist your arm and make you eat the apple. You were practically slobbering all over it before I could put it in your mouth. And don't go lying about how good I looked, when just the other day you told me that I was eating too much! As a matter of fact, *he* should be the one severely punished because he should have been there for me when I needed him. After all I am just a helpless woman."

NARRATOR: But this conversation never took place because Adam and Eve knew they had sinned against God. They accepted their punishment and were evicted out of the Garden of Eden. God still used them to help multiply the seeds of the Earth.

What if, when God told Noah to build the Ark, Noah had said—-

NOAH: "God, I can't do that. I have my reputation to think about. People know us all over town. If I build this Ark, we will be laughed at day and night. They will call us crazy and never invite us to another party again! We will be outcasts. Please don't ask me to do this. Ask anything, but don't make me be the laughingstock of the town."

NARRATOR: But Noah didn't say this. He was obedient to God, because he believed in and loved God.
What if, when God told Abraham and his family and go to a strange land, Abraham had said—-

ABRAHAM: "Can you tell me more about this place? What about my mother and father? They are old and need me. How far is it? Maybe we can come home on weekends. How long will I be gone? What about money? Will I know anybody there? Lord, why do I have to move?"

NARRATOR: But he didn't. Abraham obeyed God. He believed God and, through his obedience, became the father of many nations. And what about Sarah? We know that when God told Abraham that Sarah would have a child, she laughed. But what if she had said—-
SARAH: "Abraham, honey, listen: we are old. There just ain't no buns coming out of this oven. I know what God said, but I ain't feeling this. Let's be thankful that we are alive and have each other. Now, don't get me wrong, I don't doubt how powerful God is, but I think He missed it on this one."
NARRATOR: Of course, we all know what happened: Sarah gave birth to a beautiful baby boy. And later, God put Abraham to the test again when he asked him to sacrifice his only son, a son that God had just given them, a son whom he loved very much. What if, Abraham had said—-

ABRAHAM: "But, God, you just gave him to me. Sarah and I are too old to have more kids. We love him; we can't just give him up. Why did you give him to us only to take him back? Is this some kind of cruel joke? I am in no mood for games. Do I really know you, God?"

NAARATOR: Glory to God, Abraham was true to God. He obeyed and God promised Abraham that through his seed all nations would be blessed!
And then there was Moses. God told Moses to go Pharaoh and tell him to let God's people go. But what if, Moses had said—-

MOSES: "No disrespect to you, God, but he is the king. He's not going to listen to me. He could have me killed at the snap of his fingers. Can I at least take a few of my homeboys with me to back me up? I ain't no chicken, but Pharaoh is a bad boy. Maybe I could write him a threatening letter, thereby avoiding a lot of bloodshed; mainly, mine!"

NAARATOR: Moses stuttered his way through, and God used him to perform great miracles. God even let Moses take a few of his own homeboys: Aaron.
And we can't forget Joseph, a faithful man who refused to sin against God. But what if, when the Potiphar's wife tried to seduce Joseph time and time again, he had said—-

JOSEPH: "Maybe if I give her what she wants, she will leave me alone. Man, she sure does smell good. Potiphar has trusted me with everything else he will never know. Besides, he can have any woman he wants. This woman wants me; why not give her what she wants? Potiphar is too busy. I can consider it part of my duty, and nobody will ever know!"

NARRATOR: But Joseph said no. He refused to sin against God. Joseph was faithful to God and God was faithful to Joseph. He blessed his socks off.
And we can't forget our friend, David. David was a man after God's own heart. David didn't sin against God, but he repented. But, what if, David had tried to make excuses, and said——

DAVID: "God, I was in love. She didn't love her husband, because if she had, she wouldn't have slept with me! Besides, I am the king and what the king wants, the king gets. I know You are disappointed in me, but I am only human. I love her. I had to have her. There is nothing else I can say. We are in love."

NARRATOR: But David didn't make excuses. He repented and wrote the most beautiful Psalms ever written.
And what if the three Hebrew boys had panicked when Nebuchadnezzar was told he was to cast them into the burning furnace if they didn't worship the golden image? What if, as the fire was heated ten times hotter, those boys begin to fear and doubt?

SHEDRACH: "Ah, Meshach, that fire is putting out some serious heat. Tell me again why we want to risk our lives?"
MESHACH: "Don't go soft now. God, ah, will deliver us."
ABEDNEGO: "And we do know this, right? I mean, it is just a golden image. If we bow to it, God knows our hearts. He knows that we really serve him."
SHADRACH: "Well, if we are going to bow down, now is the time. The king is waiting, and the fire is getting hotter."
MESHACH: "Yea, maybe you guys are right. God will understand. He wouldn't want us to sacrifice our lives just to prove a point. He knows that old piece of iron means nothing to us."

ABEDNEGO: "That's right. God knows that we serve him only and we are pretending to serve the image. Let's bow down and get this over with."

NARRATOR: But praise God, they didn't bow down. They believed God would deliver them and He did.
I know we remember Ruth, the daughter-in-law of Naomi. What if, when Ruth's husband died, Ruth had treated Naomi harshly? What if she had said—

RUTH: "Your son is dead now. I will not leave you but don't be telling me what to do. You are old. You don't know anything about how to get a man. Stay out of my way and I will find someone to take care of us. I may have to break a few rules, so don't get all crazy if I do. Your son was good but he sure has lousy timing. He could have at least given me a child before he died. Oh, well, no use crying over spilled milk. Let's go find me a man!"

NARRATOR: But Ruth never said these words. She was kind and loving to her mother-in-law, and God blessed her with a fine husband and handsome son. This same son was the father of Jesse, who was the father of David.
And then there was Esther, a woman obedient to God and her uncle, Mordecai. When Mordecai heard of a terrible plot against the Jews, he sent word to Esther, who was living in the king's house, to make supplication unto the king to save them. Esther was afraid but she went to see the king. But, what if she had said—-

ESTHER: "Tell Mordecai I appreciate him taking me into his home when my mother and father died, but he doesn't own me. I am now in the king's home. There is no way I am going

to jeopardize my position here by going to see the king; you just don't barge in whenever you feel like it! And tell him not to threaten me either. I am one of the king's favorites; there is no way I am going to risk my life for people I don't even know. Tell Mordecai to be a man and go see the king himself!"
NARRATOR: Hallelujah, Esther was obedient. She proclaimed a fast and went to see the king. Esther prayed and fasted, and God touched the king's heart. The Jews were saved, their enemies defeated, and Esther became queen.
And as the saying goes, last, but certainly not least: what if the angel of the Lord appeared to Mary and told her that the Holy Ghost would come upon her and she would conceive a son; and he would be called the son of God, she had said—-

MARY: "No, not me! You see, I'm engaged to this handsome carpenter. We are in love. He is adamant about virginity. If he finds out that I am with child, he won't marry me. No, no man will. Tell God He has got to find another woman. I know a few women who don't have a man. Maybe he can use one of them. I can't lose my man. I can't do it, I just can't!"
NARRATOR: But beautiful, sweet, and gentle Mary didn't say 'not me,' she said: be it unto me according to Thy word. God honored her obedience, and she still got her man.
Hebrews 13:8 says: "Jesus Christ, the same yesterday, today, and forever. That means Jesus is still saving the lost. Let me ask you, what if Jesus asked you to accept Him as your Lord and Savior? What would your answer be? Guess what? He is asking you to accept Him as your Lord and Savior! Here are some of your answers—-"
Lord, when I stop drinking and clean myself up a bit, then I will come to You.
As soon as I get this career going, then I will concentrate on You, Lord.

I am too young. When I get older and settled down, I will come to You then, Lord.

I am so busy, working, cleaning, and raising these kids; I don't have time to go to church.

Nobody else is living right, why should I?

Do any of these excuses sound familiar? I leave you with one final question: what if God had not loved the world that he gave his only begotten son, that whosoever believeth in Him should not perish, but have everlasting life? What if God said:

GOD: "I give up! These people are hopeless. I sent a flood, I destroyed Sodom and Gomorrah, I rained fire from heaven, I came to Earth in the flesh, I died on the cross for the sins of the world. What more can I do? I wash my hands of these rebellious and hardheaded people! They are 'everything my way' kinds of people. I think I will make some robots. At least they will obey me."

But God didn't say that. He said: "Come to me; I give you my salvation. Make a choice. Who will you serve today? Have you accepted Jesus as your savior?"

Don't leave this world wondering: "WHAT IF?"